42,80

Children of Poverty

Studies and Dissertations on
the Effects of Single Parenthood,
the Feminization of Poverty,
and Homelessness

Stuart Bruchey
UNIVERSITY OF MAINE
General Editor

A Garland Series

Homeless Families

Causes, Effects, and Recommendations

Meredith van Ry

Garland Publishing, Inc.
New York & London
1993

Library of Congress Cataloging-in-Publication Data

Van Ry, Meredith, 1940–
    Homeless families : causes, effects, and recommendations / by Meredith van Ry.
        p.   cm. — (Children of poverty—studies and dissertations of the effects of
single parenthood, the feminization of poverty, and homelessness)
    Includes bibliographical references
    ISBN 0-8153-1124-9 (alk. paper)
    1. Homelessness—United States. 2. Homeless persons—United States. I. Title.
II. Series: Children of poverty.
HV4505.V36   1993
362.5'8'0973—dc20   92-35099
                                                                                              CIP

Printed on acid-free, 250-year-life paper
Manufactured in the United States of America

DEDICATION

*To homeless families throughout the world
and to their children, the truly innocent victims.*

Contents

Illustrations

TABLES

FIGURES

PREFACE

When this research was first envisioned in 1984, delays in implementation called into question whether the issue of families with young children becoming homeless would be relevant by the time the study was completed. Not only was this mistaken and optimistic thinking, but the opposite was found to be true. Families with children were actually the fastest growing segment of the homeless population in the late 1980s. Policies and programs, previously thought to be a safety net, let whole families fall through its holes and provided little assistance to help them get back on their feet and into the mainstream of society. In the 1990s, the number of homeless families continues to escalate.

To stem the increase of homeless families, this study's proposed typology on how and why families become homeless merits renewed attention. The families' suggestions require review and analysis by policy makers for strategic implementation.

ACKNOWLEDGMENTS

This project was motivated by my acquaintance with the conditions experienced by squatter families resettled outside of Delhi, India during the State of Emergency in 1975 and 1976, and the observation that governmental policies can do much to influence the families' survival and well-being.

I wish to thank to my supervisory committee; Katharine Hooper Briar, Chairperson for encouraging research regarding the plight of homeless families and to committee members Florence Stier, William Berleman, and Marsha Brown. Special recognition is also extended to Katharine Briar for the modeling and inspiration she has given through her dedicated pursuit and involvement in affecting change in social policy.

I want to express sincere appreciation to the homeless families interviewed in Seattle for sharing their personal and painful stories and for their ideas and recommendations for programs and policies pertaining to homeless families in the United States.

Heartfelt gratitude goes to my children for accepting without complaint many years of financial hardship while their mother pursued the dream of making a difference. Thanks goes also to my friends for their moral support and belief in the importance of this project.

Homeless Families

Chapter I:

Homelessness in America

"You could make it if you had a place to come home to."
- homeless mother with six children

PROBLEM STATEMENT

"Becoming homeless—no longer having a place to rest in privacy, prepare one's food, care for one's children, and store one's goods—is perhaps the most profound privation imaginable in our society" (McGerigle and Lauriat, 1983, p. xix) and one which is extremely dangerous to body, mind and spirit (National Academy of Science, 1988; Brickner, 1986; Bassuk, 1986).

Homelessness, now considered a multifaceted social welfare problem escalated in the United States during the 1980s (National Academy of Science, 1988). While the literal definition of homelessness is having no home or permanent place of residence, homelessness is characterized and defined in the literature in various ways (Miller, 1984). The descriptive definition of homelessness both identifies and categorizes persons who are regarded as homeless e.g., skid roaders, street people, alcoholics, vagrants, transients, street kids, deinstitutionalized mentally ill, bag people, etc.

Accurate counts of the homeless are difficult because it is a fluctuating and mobile population. Many researchers identify and define individuals as homeless based on the physical location where they are found. The Housing and Urban Development (HUD) report (1984) considered and counted a person as homeless if his/her night's residence was in a variety of public or private emergency shelters or any public or private space not designed for shelter e.g. cars, door ways, train stations or the street. The General Accounting Office (GAO) report used as its definition "those persons who lack resources and community ties necessary to provide for their own adequate shelter" (1985).

Shelter providers estimate that the number of homeless persons is over three million. The Alliance Housing Council estimated that there were 735,000 homeless persons on a given night and one million three hundred thousand to two million persons were homeless for one or more nights during 1988. The pervasiveness of the problem in American cities, combined with estimates of the increasing number of homeless persons in this country, led U.S. mayors to declare homelessness a crisis situation as early as 1982 (U.S. Conference of Mayors, 1982).

Factors cited to account for the current homeless problem have included chronic alcoholism and substance abuse, the deinstitutionalization of the mentally ill, and the gentrification of the inner city (Hopper & Hauberg, 1983; HUD, 1984; Kaufman, 1984). As in the 1930s, stereotypes persist which blame the homeless for their plight and claim, as does former President, Reagan, that homeless persons choose this way of life.

In the early 1980s, some argued that up to 90% of the homeless population were mentally ill (Bassuk, 1984) and that their homeless condition was the result of changes in federal laws concerning treatment of the mentally ill. The revision of mental health commitment laws in the 1960s resulted in the deinstitutionalization of thousands of mentally ill persons, returning them to their families or communities with the expectation that they would live in neighborhoods and receive needed medications and counseling from the newly instituted network of community mental health clinics (Langdon & Kass, 1985). Many of these persons never made it to the local clinics.

The revisions also prohibited institutionalizing mentally ill persons involuntarily unless they were a threat to their own or another person's life or physical safety. This prohibition prevented many mentally ill persons from ever entering the mental health system or consequently receiving the help they needed.

Many were left to fend for themselves on the streets. By the mid 1980s, emergency shelters reported that one third to one half of their residents had problems with alcoholism and/or drug abuse. Some sheltered persons were subsequently found to have a dual diagnosis of substance abuse and mental illness.

In the latter 1980s, families with children became recognized as the fastest growing segment of the increasing homeless population (National Academy of Science, 1988; National Coalition for the Homeless, 1987; U.S. Conference of Mayors, 1987). Reports stated that homeless families comprised from thirty-three (National Conference of Mayors, 1987) to forty percent (National Coalition for the Homeless, 1987; "Oklahoma's homeless," 1988) of the general homeless population. Families made up an even larger percentage of the number of homeless persons in individual cities like Seattle, Philadelphia and Portland, which claimed fifty percent or more of their homeless were families (King County Shelter Coalition, 1986; National Conference of Mayors, 1987). New York City reported that seventy-six percent of its homeless were families (National Conference of Mayors, 1987) and Yonkers, New York reported that eighty percent were families (U.S. House of Reps., 1986). Eighty percent of the homeless were also described as families in Roanoke, Virginia ("Homeless Population Increasing," 1989). The National Coalition for the Homeless reported that homelessness continued to escalate in 1989, and that the most dramatic increases (ranging to over one hundred percent) were among families ("Homeless Population Increasing", 1989).

THEORIES OF HOMELESSNESS

Several theories or models have been proposed to explain how and why people end up homeless. The causes suggested can be classified as either systemic or personal deficits, theories similar to those developed for other related social welfare problems such as unemployment and poverty (Amadei, 1987; Briar, 1986). Advocates for the homeless cite systemic reasons for homelessness, such as an inadequate or failing mental health policy, the recent recession, high unemployment rates, and the disappearance of low-income housing (Hombs & Snyder, 1983). They also criticize the federal government for failure to prevent or to respond aggressively to such problems, for cutting basic and essential social services and entitlement programs for the disadvantaged segments of our society, and for decreased federal housing funds (seventy-one percent from 1979 to 1987).

The personal deficit theory or blame the victim model was proposed by those who point to alcoholism, drug abuse, mental illness, social disaffiliation, irresponsibility, laziness or free choice of this life style to explain why people are homeless. The HUD report (1984) cites personal deficits as the primary cause of homelessness and identifies three major types of homeless persons: (1) persons with chronic disabilities such as alcoholism, drug abuse and mental illness; (2) those with severe personal crises, including battered women and runaway youth; and (3) those in adverse economic situations, such as the recently unemployed and welfare recipients. The HUD report (1984) classifies those persons who fall into the last two categories as temporarily homeless.

Bahr and Caplow (1974) suggests that social disaffiliation should not be considered a personal deficit; it may instead be the unifying element for different types of homeless persons no matter what the origin of their homelessness. Social disaffiliation, they point out, may be either internally or externally imposed; it could be the result of either the individual withdrawing from society or society withdrawing its supports during times of "socio-economic changes such as economic depressions and recessions or technical innovations that result in job displacement" (Roper, 1988, p. 121).

Between the systemic theory and personal deficit theory of homelessness, fall two additional models that explain homelessness in terms of reactions to stress and adverse changes. The victimization model posits that an accumulation of stressful events over which one has no control leaves a person helpless in combatting further life events. The vulnerability model states that inadequate coping skills and social supports leaves the individual unable to mediate between life events and outcomes.

Determining the reasons people end up homeless is judged important, because the causes or factors cited often dictate the solutions and influence attitudes regarding societal or governmental responsibility for the homeless problem (Stern, 1984).

HISTORICAL ANTECEDENTS

Homelessness is not a new phenomenon for citizens of this country nor is the size of the present homeless problem unprecedented. This country has always had a fluctuating homeless population (Arce & Vergare, 1984; Hoch, 1987). North America has had homeless tramps and hobos ("the wandering unemployed") for over one hundred years (Davis, 1984; Hoch, 1987; Leepson, 1982; Schneider, 1984; Tygiel, 1984). Almost all American cities have their own version of skid road (McSheehy, 1979; Bahr, 1973; Wallace, 1965) populated by persons stereotyped as vagrants and alcoholics but characterized by their homelessness, poverty, and acute personal problems (Baer, 1973).

Homelessness, a condition of extreme poverty, has increased dramatically during times of economic upheaval or recession (Hoch, 1987). The last time homelessness was recognized as an acute problem was during the Great Depression of the thirties (Hoch, 1987; Hopper & Hamberg, 1984; Leepson, 1982) when the homeless, including whole families, were characterized and treated by the government as transients or vagrants (Webb, 1935). The compounding and frequently sequential causes for homelessness during that period were many (Ryan, 1940):

- the downward spiraling of employment after the stock market crash in 1929;

- the mounting need for relief and the pyramiding cost of providing it;
- the flight from charitable "family relief" by many young men and boys who left the family home so that there would be "one less mouth to feed" from the limited resources;
- the frantic search for work, causing individuals and families to shift from one community to another as employment opportunities contracted;
- the return of unemployed industrial workers to family owned farms displacing tenant farm laborers;
- the uprooting of farm laborers and owners driven out by mechanical automation and economic changes;
- the exodus from the Dust Bowl caused by the great drought of 1933-1935.

HISTORY OF GOVERNMENTAL CONCERN

In the 1930s, poor relief and the provision of charity was modeled after the 1601 English Poor Laws and seen strictly as a duty to be borne by the local township, churches or private organizations. This view was reinforced by the Franklin Pierce veto of a congressional bill advocated for by social activist Dorthea Dix, which was to allow federal lands to be given to states for use in building hospitals for the mentally ill. In his veto, Pierce declared that the constitution of the United States did not give Congress the authority to take care of the "indigent insane". If it had, Congress would have the power to care for the indigent who were not insane and the federal government would be in charge of the poor of all states (Doublestein, 1986). This reinforcing of the concept of local responsibility clearly affirmed that public welfare was not a national problem. This attitude continued into the 1930s.

Up through the first four years of the Great Depression, assistance to the poor, unemployed and homeless persons was considered by the Federal government to be a local responsibility.

Local communities and private charities accepted the burden for giving relief to local residents but rejected all who lacked settlement, defined by most townships as residence in that locality, usually for one year but sometimes for as many as ten (J. Brown, 1940). Although non-residents were forced to move on, townships used up their resources as local taxes were not collectible. States were unable to provide or pass down sufficient relief. Cities and townships providing relief became bankrupt as the problem of unemployment and homelessness grew and no new money came in. They made repeated requests to Congress for financial assistance claiming that the federal government should take responsibility for its citizens, who were being affected by a national economic failure. President Hoover was adamant that it was a local responsibility and private charity would have to contribute more. He claimed the problem would soon go away as the economy recovered.

Congress responded more sympathetically. Senators Costigan and Follet repeatedly introduced bills and held hearings to support providing federal aid. A joint resolution to authorize distribution of government owned cotton and wheat to the American Red Cross passed and was not vetoed by Hoover. Since Congress could not get direct federal aid approved, a substitute bill authorizing loans to states from the federal government was introduced and passed Congress but was vetoed by Hoover because it meant an unbalanced budget. A re-introduction of an almost identical bill one week later again passed both houses and was not vetoed. Hoover later claimed that the expenditure was forced upon the government by the Democratic leaders. These loans, to be repaid with interest, were made to the governors of states upon their certification of necessity and inadequacy of resources.

On March 4, 1933, President Roosevelt took office, the Federal Emergency Relief Act (FERA) was passed and Harry Hopkins, a social worker, was appointed as its federal administrator. FERA, which operated from May 1933 to December 1935, was superseded by the Works Progress Administration (WPA), also administered by Harry Hopkins.

Both FERA and WPA provided a mass of relief programs including:

- work relief for those who could work;
- direct relief for unemployables;
- transient relief for the "unattached" person and later for whole families;
- special programs for the rural population which included a resettlement program for farm families who were moved from non-arable land to more productive areas.

Relief consisted of cash, in-kind benefits such as medical care and clothing made in the WPA programs. Work programs were seen both as a means of assistance to the unemployed and as a way to prime the pump of industry. In order to provide work to some unemployed academicians and professionals, programs were developed to use their talents teaching classes such as literacy, music and art to the public.

The federal government sponsored research on the homeless and the effects of the Depression on the population during the 1930s, through the WPA. Statistics were kept which document the number and type of relief services that were used by the transient unemployed (Webb, 1935), the urban workers on relief (Palmer & Wood, 1936), rural families on relief (Zimmerman & Whetten, 1938) and migrant families (Webb & Brown, 1938). Government reports also documented rural migration in the United States during the Depression (Lively & Taeuber, 1939) and chronicled the Federal Emergency Relief Administration (Carothers, 1937).

As a safeguard to prevent the extreme hardships of the Depression from recurring, the federal Social Security Act was passed in 1935. The Social Security Act provided a national insurance system for retirement, and disability, with federal grants to states to help with old age assistance, aid to dependent children and income for the blind. The insurance program was later extended to provide benefits for dependents and survivors of those receiving the federal benefits (Merriam, 1971; Kammerman and Kahn, 1976; Steiner, 1966). In speaking of families and family services, Beatt said, "the Social Security Act established the principle that the responsibility for meeting basic maintenance needs of families is a governmental one" (1971, p. 394).

The Social Security Act of 1935 was not designed to eliminate all vestiges of poverty. Instead, it was intended to provide federal matching grants to states enacting programs of public assistance to the categories covered by the federal act (Steiner, 1966). The states determined who qualified for the benefits and the level of support. Old Age, Survivors, Disability, and Health Insurance (OASDHI) relied on worker/employer contributions, and the government merely administered it. Homelessness was not eradicated for many on skid road (Bahr, 1973; Hoch, 1987), although articles reporting its decline appeared in the late 1960s (Bahr, 1967).

Studies on homelessness during the 1960s and 1970s concentrated primarily on the inhabitants of skid row and found them to be disaffiliated with alcohol their chief pathology (Bahr, 1967; 1973). The early skid row studies which focused on the male alcoholic, reinforced the stereotypes of the homeless hobo or vagrant as both disaffiliated and deviant. Other research examined the issues of disaffiliation and alcoholism in women on skid row (Bahr & Garrett, 1976; Corrigan, 1984; Crystal, 1984) and the problems of homeless women in general, with mixed findings (Hagen & Ivanoff, 1987; Stoner, 1983).

HOMELESSNESS IN THE 1980s

The magnitude of the resurgent homeless problem developing in the 1980s, was recognized as increasing numbers of homeless people appeared living on the streets, in public places, in cars, under bridges, or requesting emergency shelter in both large cities and small communities (HUD, 1984). Research was undertaken to gain some understanding of the magnitude, causes and contributing factors of this phenomenon and the types of persons who are now homeless (GAO, 1985; HUD, 1984;

National Academy of Sciences, 1988). Local service agencies, coalitions, task forces, or local governments undertook studies or commissioned research to investigate claims concerning the size and condition of the homeless problem and the requisite need for more funding for services. The studies indicated that the homeless population of the 1980s was different from the long held image of the typical homeless person as an older white alcoholic male (Hagen & Ivanoff, 1988; Homelessness Information Exchange, 1988; Leepson, 1982). The new population was found to be more heterogeneous (Bingham, Green, White, 1987; Hagen, 1987; Robertson, 1986; Phillips, DeChillo, Kronenfeld & Middleton-Jeter, 1988; Hombs & Snyder, 1984). In addition, these reports indicated a larger percentage of minorities, families, single women (Hagen & Ivanoff, 1988; Stoner, 1983) and a younger population, with the average age being thirty-four years (HUD, 1984; GAO, 1985). The generation of this new heterogeneous homeless population has been attributed to a variety of factors.

Because many of the persons observed living on the street or sheltered in missions or in public places appeared to be mentally ill, the National Institute of Mental Health funded major research studies (Roth & Bean, 1985). The deinstitutionalization of mentally ill patients, since the mid 1960s, turned thousands of persons out into communities unprepared to care for them (Goldman & Morrissey, 1985; Hopper, 1983; Lamb, 1984; Mc Gerigle & Louriat, 1983; Rhoden, 1984). Nontreatment for the mentally ill resulted in their homelessness or residence in cheap hotels (Arce & Vergare, 1984; Goldman & Morrissey, 1985; Wolch and Gabriel, 1985).

Other factors cited to explain the increase of homeless persons include a recessionary economy, high unemployment (Snow, Baker, Anderson, & Martin, 1986), reforms in laws and cutbacks in social services (Frazier, 1985; Hoch, 1987; Hombs & Snyder, 1984; Jirovec, 1984). Despite the rhetoric of a social safety net, cutbacks in federal welfare programs by the Reagan Administration were substantial (Jirovec, 1984; Wolch & Gabriel, 1985). Federal housing budget cuts and urban renewal displaced both the elderly, with minimal resources, and other marginally surviving persons from low-income housing (Human Resources Coalition, 1984).

Juvenile justice laws, changed to insure that juveniles were treated as fairly or equally as adults, allowed "runaway" or "throwaway" youth to attempt survival on the streets, where they often turned to crime or prostitution to survive (Subcommittee on the Constitution, 1980; Sullivan & Damrosch, 1987). Many homeless women and adolescent females reported leaving their homes after repeated abuse (Hagen, 1987; Stefl, 1987; Stoner, 1983) adding to the swell of persons requesting emergency shelter.

Several of the studies, undertaken primarily to investigate the incidence and problems of the homeless mentally ill, discovered homeless families in public shelters or living in cars or tents (Brown, MacFarland, Paredes & Stark, 1983; Roth & Bean, 1985). Little research was undertaken to determine the incidence or particular problems of homeless families (Bassuk, 1986, 1987; Miller, 1986). Most studies which looked at homeless families focused on the abominable living conditions in New York "welfare hotels" (Coalition for the Homeless, 1984; Kozel, 1988a, 1988b, 1988c; Simpson, Kilduff & Blewett, 1984; Wackstein, 1983, 1984).

The problem of homeless families has been growing across the country (GAO, 1985; HUD, 1984; National Academy of Science, 1988). The cutbacks in social programs and entitlements along with high rates of unemployment pushed low-income people deeper into poverty, out of their homes and apartments (Hopper, 1985) and forced them to live in public shelters, in abandoned buildings (Borgos, 1984; Leavitt & Seagert, 1984), under bridges and freeways, in parking garages, over grates and heating vents, in bus or subway stations, in cars and in tent cities, or on the street (Hombs and Snyder, 1984).

That homelessness is a serious social welfare issue is beyond question. Homelessness in the United States threatens the very survival needs of the approximately three million persons who experience it (Hombs & Snyder, 1983). Being without shelter or the resources to acquire it compromises physical welfare and leads to a multitude of health problems (Brickner, 1985).

Without a permanent address, homeless people have difficulty qualifying for such social service benefits as public housing, food stamps and medical care, and are forced to depend on handouts to eat and emergency shelters to sleep. The state-wide Ohio study funded by the National Institute of Mental Health stated that a —homeless person's mental health status is negatively affected by virtue of being homeless (Roth & Bean, 1985). A great deal of the mental depression reported in studies of the homeless mentally ill was found to be situationally caused, rather than organic, and exacerbated by homelessness. The experience of homelessness is devastating to a persons psychological well being (Bassuk, 1986, 1987; Lamb, 1984). As destructive as homelessness is to the adult, it is an even more serious problem for children (Bassuk, 1985; Gewirtzman & Fodor, 1987; National Academy of Science, 1988). Homeless children suffer physically, mentally and socially (Hayes, 1984; League of Women Voters of Seattle, 1985; Miller, 1986; Wackstein, 1983, 1984; Wright & Weber, 1987). Welfare Hotel studies indicated that frequently school age children were not enrolled in or attending school and those attending were often discriminated against ("Homeless children denied," 1988; Gewirtzman & Fodor, 1987). The Education Department estimated that more than 65,000 homeless school age children did not attend school regularly. The National Coalition for the Homeless claimed that these numbers were based on an undercount of homeless children and that the problem was actually much larger (Washington Post News Service, 1989).

→   Although there have been many studies undertaken to count or at least arrive at an estimate of the number of homeless people in this country, researchers acknowledge that methodologically this is a very difficult population to locate or count (Wiegard, 1985). Most estimates of the number of homeless are derived from usage and requests for emergency shelters and the concomitant turn-aways. Because the majority of shelters are geared to the single adult male, this is the population which has been most studied. The concerns and even the counts of homeless youth and families have often been neglected. Youth are considered dependents of either their parents or of the state and therefore have a home whether or not they chose to use it.

Families, if by chance homeless, have been considered only temporarily so; homeless families with children have been viewed as an anomaly. Because government has provided grants such as AFDC to take care of a family's emergency needs, discussion about the dire situation of families in poverty has been dismissed as already being dealt with.

On account of families with children becoming homeless in increasing numbers and being especially vulnerable to the ravages of homelessness, some research was undertaken (Miller, 1986). Bassuk, Rubin and Lauriat (1986) studied the mental health of women and children in emergency shelters and Miller and Linn (1987) reported on the health status of children in sheltered families. Maza and Hall (1988) undertook a preliminary study on homeless children and their families, through the Travelers Aid Society. Johnson (1989) reported the demographics of families staying in Salvation Army shelters in St. Louis. All authors reported that the situation was serious and additional research was necessary to both fill the gaps in knowledge and to call attention to the problem.

Policy makers and service providers alike need specific information to develop social policy and service programs to prevent or ameliorate conditions which allow families to become homeless. Data about the demographics of the homeless family population and the etiology and effects of homelessness on both the family and individual family members is required. An exploration of the utilization of existing social services is needed to ascertain the adequacy and appropriateness of present policies and services. Recommendations made by homeless families, themselves, for services and policy changes is also considered germane.

PURPOSE OF STUDY

This study was undertaken to explore the etiology of homelessness for families in the 1980's and to investigate the effects of homelessness on family members including the children. Governmental supports are available to families through the Social Security Act and its amendments, which include Aid to Families with Dependent Children, Medicaid, Food Stamps and Public Housing. The fact that families with children actually become homeless in this country has confused the public and mystified government officials. Local communities and society at large acknowledge some responsibility for the well being and education of their children. The lack of data on why the existing supports are not adequate to prevent families from becoming homeless has hampered efforts to prevent or solve this problem.

Much of the research on homeless persons, including homeless families, involves analyzing depersonalized data collected on the intake forms of emergency shelters. The intent of this study was to delve deeper into the problem and to personally interview homeless families. The goal was to find out from them, in their own words, who they are, how they became homeless, what could have prevented it and their recommendations for needed services and policies.

This research was directed specifically to explore the following subject areas:

1. The sequence of events that leads families with young children to become homeless.
2. The measures taken by families to prevent or ward off homelessness.
3. Gender and age related effects of homelessness on families.
4. Difficulties reported by family caregivers while homeless.
5. Intervention services needed to address and ameliorate the stresses and suffering experienced by homeless families.
6. Identification of transitional services required to stabilize families in home and community.
7. Implications for multi-level policies needed to prevent homelessness and the problems resulting from families becoming homeless.

Chapter II:

Methodology

RESEARCH DESIGN

An exploratory, cross-sectional survey design was used to elicit information regarding the multiple causes, effects and possible solutions for the complex problems of homeless families with young children. The survey instrument was designed to collect information in a semi-structured format and included both pre-coded and open-ended questions. Participants in the study were expected to have particular knowledge of the problems of homeless families based on their own experience and that of their peers and homeless acquaintances.

SAMPLE SITE SELECTION

The study was conducted in Seattle, Washington. In this city, as in most cities throughout the country, homeless families can be found on downtown streets, living in cars, in city or county parks, doubled up with relatives or friends, in soup kitchens, food bank lines, hospital emergency waiting rooms and in shelters for the homeless. Although all of the above locations were considered as a source of participants for this study, most of these sites were also the location of people not homeless. In order to obtain the maximum number of homeless families without causing them the embarrassment of being identified and singled

out from the crowd, the researcher decided to interview families
living in emergency shelters especially designated for homeless
families with children.

In 1987, Seattle had twelve to fifteen programs that helped
shelter homeless families for one or more nights. Some programs
fluctuated in size and went in and out of service as their resources,
primarily donations, varied. At least five of the programs provided
vouchers and made referrals for nightly or weekly
accommodations in local motels or other emergency shelters.
Seven to nine of the programs provided shelter in their own
facilities such as apartments or vacant houses donated or rented
for short periods of time. Two shelter programs were considered
"safe houses" for women and children escaping domestic
violence; their locations were kept confidential. One program
consisted of a single family residence that sheltered one family at a
time. Two programs rented houses or apartments for homeless
families as their resources and donations permitted. Another
program sheltered two or three families in a former convent for up
to three months. The largest shelter program, housing fifty-six
families at a time, was run as a Christian gospel mission. This
shelter did not allow outsiders on their premises to contact,
interview or provide services to their residents.

Homeless families move from shelter to shelter if their
situations have not improved enough to get into regular housing
by the time their allotted length of stay in a shelter is exhausted.
One goal of the research design was to avoid or reduce the
problems inherent in trying to access and interview families in
multiple programs of varying size, constraints, location and
lengths of stay. Two programs were identified that served a
sufficient number of families and allowed them a long enough stay
to provide the researcher the possibility of accessing a large
number of families to interview and yet turned over frequently
enough to allow additional families to interview, if necessary. The
smaller of these two shelter programs housed fifteen single parent,
female headed families for approximately three weeks. Priority
was given to victims of family violence who were in immediate
need of shelter. The facility consisted of the lower three floors of
an enclosed security type apartment building with the outside

doors kept locked for safety reasons. The larger shelter accommodated up to thirty-one homeless one or two parent families at a time for up to a month. They gave priority to larger families in need who seemed appropriate, were not substance abusers and had verifiable information. The thirty-one apartments were individual units, each with their own separate outside entrance. Permission was granted by the boards of each shelter to conduct the survey and interview the families at these two shelters.

SURVEY INSTRUMENT

A review of the literature on homeless families revealed no previously designed and tested instruments which could be used to answer the questions of interest. Intake forms used by emergency shelters for homeless families were found to be inadequate for the purposes of this study due to their brevity. Hence, a survey instrument was designed specifically for this project.

The findings in the existing literature on homeless single adults suggested some basic issues to investigate as they relate to homeless families (Bahr, 1973; Bassuk, 1986; Baxter & Hooper, 1984; Lamb, 1984). These issues included the incidence of mental illness, substance abuse, prior and present health problems, alienation from relatives and friends, and physical or domestic violence. Questions on issues specifically related to homeless children, such as school attendance and behavioral changes for both school age and preschool children, and inquiries addressing the etiology of homelessness for each participant family, were added. Through open-ended questions, families were given the opportunity to make recommendations for program or policy changes they considered necessary to prevent families from becoming homeless. They were also encouraged to give suggestions regarding the help they thought was needed to ameliorate the problems and effects resulting in and from being homeless. (See appendix)

A draft of the instrument was reviewed by the staff of two homeless family shelters. Suggestions were made for changes in wording which would make the questions more understandable and relevant to their clients. After those recommended changes were incorporated, a social worker who served homeless families in other shelter programs was asked to critique the instrument again for any further modifications necessary.

A final draft of the instrument and consent form was submitted to the managers of the two shelters where the interviews would take place. Shelter staff were protective of the families and concerned that the families' situations and personal need for validation be recognized and respected. They stipulated that each family who participated in the study be paid ten dollars for their time and trouble by the researcher. This was agreed upon. A final copy of the instrument and consent form along with letters of agreement from the shelters was then submitted to the University of Washington Human Subjects Review Board. (See appendix) Approval of the instrument was granted.

PARTICIPANT SAMPLE SELECTION

All resident families in the two shelters at the time of the study were sought as participants for the study. Each shelter determined its own method of letting their residents know about the research project and of the open invitation to participate. Shelter A, the smaller shelter, had a weekly meeting which all residents were required to attend. It was at these meetings that an announcement of the study was made and a sign up sheet was passed around to be signed by anyone willing to be interviewed. The researcher was later given the names and room numbers of the potential interviewees.

At Shelter B, the larger shelter, new families coming into the program were informed of the research project at the beginning of their stay. If interested, they were asked to schedule a time for the interview convenient for them through the office staff. Families who were already in residence at the shelter were told of the study when they made contact with the shelter staff at the office for other reasons e.g., requesting supplies, bus tokens, use of the phone, etc. Interviews were then coordinated through the office staff and scheduled when a meeting room or office would be otherwise vacant. The researcher was later informed of the time for the scheduled interviews.

Information about the research project seemed to reach the families in Shelter B in a sporadic and haphazard way due to more pressing issues and concerns at the time of their contact with office staff. Staff members subsequently suggested that the researcher make up a small flyer that could be posted on the bulletin board or passed out to residents. The staff members suggested that the possibility of earning ten dollars be featured since the holidays were approaching and most families had no money and would want to buy presents for their children. The staff sincerely wanted to assist both the families and the researcher. Copies of the flyer were also given to Shelter A.

Interviews began the first week of December, 1987. An attempt was made to interview one hundred percent of the families who would stay in each shelter that month. The number was estimated to be approximately fifty to sixty families. This was thought to be enough for the purposes of the study. However, water drainage problems made two apartments uninhabitable in Shelter A. Necessary cleaning and repairs kept several apartments out of service in Shelter B. By the twenty-third of December all available families at both shelters had been interviewed, a total of only thirty-nine families. Since it was the holiday season and the weather was cold, concessions were made on the usual stay limitations and no family was required to move out of either shelter until after the first week of the new year. The decision was made to wait a month, until there was a complete turnover of residents, before interviewing again.

Thirty homeless families were interviewed at Shelter B, during the month of February. Because Shelter B provided an adequate number of additional one and two parent families, no more families were interviewed at Shelter A. Some residents at both shelters were missed during the month of December and at Shelter B during the month of February. During the month of

February, a staff person at the second shelter agreed to list the family composition, number of persons, ages, and race for all families not interviewed at that shelter during the month of February and the previous month of December.

After the fact, it was discovered that at Shelter B a total of nineteen families were missed, twelve in the month of December and seven in February, ten single-parent families and nine two-parent households. Two families were not scheduled because they spoke no English and ten families because their stays were too short. Three families did not have any time available which coincided with the times when the interviews were possible. One family did not want to be interviewed because they did "not want any attachment to homelessness". Three families that were scheduled for interviews did not show up. At Shelter A, no record of families not interviewed was kept.

INTERVIEW PROCEDURE

All interviews were conducted by the researcher. At Shelter A, the smaller shelter for women and children, the researcher/interviewer would go to the building, ring the door bell, identify herself and be let in. The researcher would then go to the office and get a list of three to four persons who expressed willingness to be interviewed. The staff would look up apartment numbers and give them to the researcher who would then knock on doors until one of the designated residents was found in her apartment. Often the family was out of the building "taking care of business".

After using this method for four days with limited success, the researcher was told by the shelter staff to just knock on any apartment door, introduce herself, explain the purpose of the research and proceed with the interview if the resident had time and was willing to participate. This proved more fruitful and resulted in a total of thirteen interviews at this shelter, one of which was with a single woman with grown and emancipated children. Although not the subject of this study, she requested an interview to talk about the dire situation of single homeless women, which she felt was much worse than that of single women with children. This interview was kept separate from those of the families.

At Shelter B, the larger family shelter, contacts between family adults and the researcher were made through the intermediary of shelter staff. Appointments were scheduled by the staff only at the times a meeting room or office was available, since the staff considered the apartment complex too dangerous for the researcher or any outsider to visit due to several recent rapes in the area.

The researcher met the family head of household, either the adult female or the male or both, in the shelter office, then went with them to the meeting room across the street for the interview. Children frequently accompanied their parents if there was no one else with whom to leave them. At the start of each interview, the study was explained and all questions answered. The consent form was read and signed by the participants. A copy of the instrument was given to the respondents to follow along with while the researcher read the questions aloud and wrote the answers. The participants were informed that they could skip answering any question they felt uncomfortable with or didn't want to answer.

Most families voluntarily reported that the interview was a very positive experience and thanked the researcher for the opportunity to talk about their situation. One mother of four children said she thought the experience was as valuable as counseling or therapy. A male respondent interrupted the researcher one quarter of the way through his interview to say that he had used an alias when introducing himself because he was skeptical about the real purpose of the study. He wanted to correctly identify himself later on in the interview because the questions being asked were "so right on" and nothing to be afraid of.

At the close of the interview, each participating family was given a ten dollar bill. Most families said they appreciated the money and stated that it would be used for necessities like doing the laundry, gas, additional food, disposable diapers, toilet paper, or other sundries such as shampoo, soap, sanitary napkins, deodorant, and cleaning supplies. One single mother of four refused the money when she found out that it was coming out of the researcher's pocket and not from a grant. Yet another mother handed the ten dollar bill to her five year old son so he would have some money to spend. Several respondents asked whether the other adult family member not present could be paid ten dollars for a separate interview.

ANALYSIS

Data were coded and analyzed for each variable. Descriptive statistics such as frequencies, means, medians, modes and standard deviations were used when appropriate. Answers to open-ended questions were collapsed and coded using content analysis techniques for drawing categories from qualitative data (Miles & Huberman, 1984; Orenstein & Phillips, 1978). For those coded questions where a large percentage of the answers fell into the "other or unique" category, a more detailed analysis or listing was undertaken.

Chapter III:

Population Characteristics

"I couldn't believe all the people that were homeless at the mission."

- Native American homeless mother

DEMOGRAPHICS

Household composition

Interviews were conducted with sixty-eight families that included 190 children. In the study, thirty-four (50%) of the families were headed by single females, three (4%) were headed by single males, and thirty-two (46%) were two-parent households. Two families had an extra adult female relative staying with them. The number of children in the homeless families ranged from one to seven, with three the average. Not all children lived with their parents; eight families (12%) were split up, with half of the children living with relatives, friends, or in state-sponsored foster care.

Ages

The parents' ages ranged from eighteen to forty-six years, with the mean age for the adult females twenty-nine years and for adult males thirty-one. One forty-nine year old grandmother was in the shelter with her grandchildren. Forty-seven of the children (25%) in the study were under three years of age, and fifty-two

(27%) between three and six years old. Ninety-one (48%) of the children were school aged, six to nineteen years old.

Ethnicity

The population contained a mixture of ethnic groups. In the population as a whole, forty-seven (47%) of the adults were Caucasian, forty-one (41%) African-American, six (6%) Native American, five (5%) Latino and two (2%) Hawaiian. Sixty-three (33%) of the children were Caucasian, eighty-seven (46%) African-American, nine (5%) Native American, six (3%) Latino and seven (4%) Hawaiian. Nineteen (10%) of the children are reported by their mothers to be an equal mix of two races, usually Caucasian and African-American.

Education

The educational level of ninety-eight of the one-hundred and one adults in the sample was reported. Twenty-five (24%) completed junior high school or some high school before quitting. Sixty-eight (69%) had a high school diploma, GED certificate, vocational training or some college. Six (6%) were university graduates, two with master's degrees.

Geographic origin

In many cities it is believed that the homeless population in their area are primarily migrants from other parts of the country, who come to their area for a handout. In this study, it was found that the majority of families, thirty-nine (57%), were residents of Washington State before becoming homeless. Twenty-four of those families were from Seattle, twelve from King County and three from nearby municipalities. Twenty-nine families (43%) reported that they lived in another state prior to becoming homeless. They explained that as their situation became untenable due to negative circumstances, such as a recent or imminent loss of job, domestic violence, or drug abuse and crime in their immediate environment, they decided to do something about it, to leave. This move preceded and precipitated their homelessness, when, after arriving, they were not able to find affordable housing or jobs. Forty-nine families (73%) lived only in Washington State at the time of and since becoming homeless. Some of the other twenty-seven percent were living in the state when they became homeless, moved to see if they could find a job or get temporary help from relatives or friends in another state, then came back. A few families from out of state became homeless in the process of traveling from state to state following job leads.

When the families were asked the primary reason they chose to relocate or move to this area, forty families, who were not originally native to the area, responded. Fourteen families (35%), thirteen of them single parents, reported they came to Seattle to be closer to relatives or friends, nine families (22%) were looking for or had been promised a job, eight (20%) said they chose Seattle because they were previous residents and liked it here. Five families (12%) said they moved to this area to escape domestic violence or drug problems in their community. Two families were just passing through when they ran out of money. Only one homeless family, a single women with twin babies, said she moved to Seattle because she "heard they helped out homeless more."

Table 1. Reasons families originally moved to this area

Reason	Frequency	Percent
Family or friends in area	14	35%
Looking for or promised job	9	22%
Previous residents	8	20%
Fleeing abuse	5	12%
Passing through	2	5%
Seattle helps more	1	2%

n=40

Time in shelter

All but seven families had been in the shelter where they were interviewed for less than one month. Several families were interviewed on their first or second day. The average time in the shelter was one to two weeks and for twenty-seven families (40%) this shelter was the first one they had ever used. Eighteen families (26%) reported doubling-up with friends or relatives prior to taking refuge in an emergency shelter. Twenty-two (32%) families responding to this question took residence in an emergency shelter less than one week after becoming homeless. Twenty-two (32%) families said they found space in a shelter one week to one month after losing housing. Another twenty-two families (32%) took from one month to over one year before they used emergency shelters. In three years, the 68 families accumulated a total of one hundred fifty-four separate stays in shelters or doubling-up with relatives or friends, an average of more than two per family. The number increased to four when those who said this was their first stay are subtracted.

When asked how long it had been since they were last in a house or apartment which they considered home, the times varied considerably from the times given for the intervals from becoming homeless until they used a shelter. This can be explained by the fact that many families spent time after losing housing doubled up with relatives which delayed their need for emergency shelter. Other families stayed in motels, camped out, or lived in their car until that no longer worked. Some families were found to spend time in an emergency shelter, then move in with relatives or friends for a while, then back to a shelter. Two families had been homeless for two and a half to three years.

Shelter need

Only nine families (13%), felt that a one month stay in a shelter would be sufficient time to enable them to go to regular or permanent housing. Sixteen families (23%) thought six weeks was the minimum time necessary. Eleven families (16%) believed they would need two to three months. Seven families (10%) said they would need more than three months. Twelve families (18%) reported they would need emergency shelter until low-income housing was available. Six families (9%) thought they would need shelter only until they received their first public assistance check or had found a job. Seven families (10%) with especially difficult or complicated situations could not give an estimate of how long it would take them to be able to move into permanent housing.

EMPLOYMENT AND FINANCIAL ISSUES

"The worst thing after not having a place or food is not having anything to do."

- single father of two

Income prior to homelessness

The families reported a monthly income before becoming homeless ranging from $0 for four families to over $4000 for two professional couples. The mean income was $1073.57 with a standard deviation of $906.96. Thirty-one families (48%) received all of their income from employment and eight families (12%) from a combination of employment and government grants. Nineteen families (28%) received their income from AFDC grants and four families (6%) from either disability insurance or other governmental programs.

Thirty-nine families (57%) were able to pay their bills on a regular basis before becoming homeless; twenty-eight families (41%) reported they were not. Forty-nine families (72%) had used some private or governmental assistance programs prior to becoming homeless; nineteen families (28%) had not. Of the various programs available twenty-nine families (43%) used food banks and fifteen families (22%) had used a one-time utility assistance program. Most families said they did not know the latter program was available.

Present income

The income of families in the shelter ranged from a low of $0 for twenty-six families (38%) to a high of $1100. The mean income was $369.66 with a standard deviation of $366.43. Of the forty-two families with income, thirteen families (30%) received income from employment and one family (2%) from a combination of both employment and AFDC. Twenty-two (52%) families received income from AFDC, two families (5%) from unemployment compensation and four families (12%) from other governmental programs.

Type of work

Twenty-nine adult females (45%) described their regular kind of work as service jobs. Ten (15%) reported clerical work, and four each in professional jobs, manual labor, and technical jobs. Eleven mothers (17%) said, prior to becoming homeless, they had only been homemakers. While at the shelter, four females were employed outside the family; sixty females (92%) were not. One mother was on leave from her job until she could get her family back into regular housing.

Manual labor was the regular kind of work for fifteen males (44%); for nine (26%), it was service industry jobs; for four (12%), technical work; and for three (9%), professional jobs. Fifteen adult males (44%) were employed while living in the shelter; nineteen (56%) were not.

Table 2. Regular type of work

Females n=65

Jobs	Frequency	Percent
Service	29	45%
Manual	4	6%
Clerical	10	15%
Professional	4	6%
Technical	4	6%
Other	3	5%
Homemakers	11	17%

Males n=34

Jobs	Frequency	Percent
Service	9	26%
Manual	15	44%
Professional	3	9%
Technical	4	12%
Other	3	9%

Childcare utilization

Thirty-eight families (57%), more than half, had never used daycare for their children. Twenty-one families (31%) used a daycare previously and five families (7%) said they used relatives to care for their children. Three families (4%) reported they had never used daycare and were afraid to, because of recent newspaper stories and publicity about sexual abuse of children in daycare centers.

Chapter IV:

Becoming Homeless

"We lost our housing for a combination of reasons."
- family with four children

CONTRIBUTING FACTORS

In order to prevent homelessness for families, it is important to be aware of its causes; but in addition to understanding the common problems, being aware of differences may provide tools to help prevent homelessness. This chapter aims at both.

Most significant problem

The families were asked to list three most significant problems that contributed to their loss of housing. Although they cite the same problems as primary, secondary and tertiary causal factors, no family listed the same problem more than once. Each family ranked the importance of similar problems differently. "No job" was reported to be the most significant problem for eighteen families (26%); for some families their lack of job is due to medical conditions, such as a back injury, leg problems, stomach ulcers, cancer, and pregnancies. Fourteen families (21%) listed "no money" as their most pivotal problem and six families (9%) reported domestic violence as the primary problem. For another six families (9%) it was substance abuse in the immediate family. Five families (7%) cited problems involving a primary relationship such as divorce, separation, a cancelled marriage plan, and problems with boyfriends. Four families (6%) reported the most significant problem which caused their homelessness was with relatives or friends and caused by the overcrowded conditions of doubling-up. In one case, overcrowding resulted in six children having to stay in one bedroom. (Doubling up was not seen by these families as a consequence or stage of homelessness but as a way of dealing with a temporary problem. For some families, relatives are considered morally responsible to take in family members and to help them until they get past the problem. Friends are considered quasi-family with quasi-obligations.) Fifteen families (22%) had other, unique problems which they considered the principal factors contributing to their loss of housing.

When single parents were looked at separately, the positions and importance of each of the above problems changes. No money was cited first by seven (22%) of the thirty-seven single parent families. Domestic violence, and substance abuse tied for second place as contributing to homelessness for single parent families. Each factor was cited as the primary problem by six (16%) families. No job was listed first as a causal factor by four (11%) single parents. Complications caused by relationships and doubling-up were each said to be primary problems for four (11%) families. Other, unique problems were cited first by six (16%) single-parent families.

Table 3a-3d. Most significant problems ranked by families as contributing to their homelessness

3a. Primary Problem/All Families n=68

Problem	Frequency	Percent
No job	18	26%
No money	14	21%
Domestic violence	6	9%
Substance abuse	6	9%
Relationships	5	7%
Doubling-up	4	6%
Other/ Unique	15	22%

3b. Primary Problem/Single Parents   n=37

Problem	Frequency	Percent
No money	7	22%
Domestic violence	6	16%
Substance abuse	6	16%
No job	4	11%
Relationships	4	11%
Doubling-up	4	11%
Other/ Unique	6	16%

Secondary problem

Sixty families listed a second factor which contributed to
their homelessness. Twenty families (34%) cited either no money
or financial problems; twelve families (20%) the lack of a job.
Five families (8%) cited eviction. Another five families (8%)
reported doubling-up with relatives or friends, in response to
losing their housing, did not work and was, itself, a problem.
Another family thought their second most significant problem was
that they had no relatives or friends to move in with. Eighteen
families (30%) indicated other, unique problems as the second
problem contributing to their loss of housing. These problems
included an abusive relationship, substance abuse, lack of low-
income housing, a lack of childcare, not receiving child support,
feeling in danger in their previous housing, having two step-sons
precipitously move in with them in a small apartment, unpaid
water and electric bills from previous tenants, and problems with
the landlord. Eight families (12%) did not list a second problem.

3c.   Secondary Problem/All Families   n=60

Problem	Frequency	Percent
No money	20	34%
No job	12	20%
Eviction	5	8%
Doubling-up	5	8%
Other/Unique	18	30%
(e.g. lack of childcare, welfare cut off)		

Tertiary problem

Thirty-six families indicated a third problem contributing to their homelessness. Eight (22%) pointed to lack of money or financial problems. Six families (17%) thought their third problem was having no relative or friend to turn to or stay with. The third problem for four (11%) families was eviction. Not having a job and no low-income housing available were each cited by three (8%) families. Two families reported doubling-up with relatives as their third problem. Ten families (28%) cited unique factors such as medical problems, lack of life skills, an employer filing for bankruptcy, and not being able to get housing due to bad references. Thirty-two families (47%) did not cite a third problem.

3d. Tertiary Problem/All Families   n=36

Problem	Frequency	Percent
No money	7	19%
No family to help	6	17%
Eviction	4	11%
No job	3	8%
No low-income housing	3	8%
Doubling up	2	5%
Other/ Unique	10	28%

- No family listed the same problem more than once.
- Not all families listed a second or third problem.
- Percentages given are tabulated from those who responded.

DOMESTIC OR PERSONAL PROBLEMS

Physical health problems

The families were asked if they had prior health problems that may have affected their ability to solve their housing quandary. Thirty families (44%) replied affirmatively. Eight families (12%) reported health problems experienced by mothers, six (9%) by fathers, seven (10%) by children, four (6%) by other family members, and in five families (7%) by more than one person. In responding to questions on how health problem affected the family's well being, fourteen families (52%) said that their time, especially time away from the job, was affected. Sixteen families (60%) reported health problems affected them financially and eighteen (66%) claimed dealing with family illness took a lot of their energy. They reported that the toll taken on their time, finances and energy directly or indirectly affected their housing stability.

Mental illness or emotional problems

The families were asked about the presence of mental illness or emotional problems both before and after becoming homeless. They were also asked whether mental illness or the emotional problems of a family member affected their ability to cope with or keep housing. Forty-six families (68%) reported that neither problem was present in their family prior to becoming homeless. Twenty-two families (32%) indicated a problem with emotions before they became homeless but said the problem was situationally caused. Seven families claimed they experienced stress and depression related to either their loss of jobs or deteriorating financial situation. Two families said their depression was the result of the death of a baby or young child in their family. Thirteen families reported conditions such as domestic violence or not getting along with family members caused them emotional problems. In five families, depression and stress was complicated by their own or others' alcohol or drug use.

Divorce to homelessness

To explore one of the reasons suggested for women and children becoming homeless, the families were asked whether divorce was a problem that contributed to their becoming homeless. Twenty-seven (73%) of the thirty-seven single parent families report that divorce was not a factor; ten (37%) reply that it was, including one male single parent. He reported that he and his children were homeless as a direct result of his having to assume the full responsibility for his four children after his wife left them. A second male single parent said divorce was not the immediate cause of homelessness for him and his children but it contributes significantly to the problem.

Domestic violence/abuse

The families were asked specifically, if domestic violence or abuse was a problem for their families. Forty-seven families (69%) responded that it was not; twenty-one (31%) responded that it was. These numbers later changed. When the data were separated and analyzed for single parent families, nineteen families (51%) responded that domestic violence was not a problem, and eighteen families (49%) reported that it was. Three of the two-parent families reported a domestic violence problem in their family.

When the families were asked how long the abuse or violence had been going on, two additional families, one two-parent and one single-parent, admitted it as a problem bringing the total to twenty-three families. The abuse lasted for less than six months for four families (17%), for six months to one year for two families (9%), and for one to two years for another two families (9%). Three families (13%) acknowledged their abuse continuing for two to three years. For seven families (30%) the abuse was reported to have gone on from three to five years and for four families (17%) from five to twelve years. One woman could not remember how long it had been going on.

Table 4. Length of time family endured domestic violence

Time	Frequency	% of families	% of abused
No problem	45	66%	0%
< 6 mo	4	6%	17%
6 mo - 1 yr	2	3%	9%
1 yr - 2 yr	2	3%	9%
2 yr - 3 yr	3	4%	13%
3 yr - 5 yr	7	10%	30%
5 yr - 12 yr	4	6%	17%
Can't remember	1	1%	4%

The families were asked if family violence or abuse was the reason they sought emergency shelter. Sixteen families responded that it was. Two families said it was partly the reason they became homeless and sought shelter.

Twenty-four families reported particular factors or events seemed related to an increase of violence by the abuser. Thirteen (54%) families said alcohol or drug use appeared to be a causative factor for increased violence. For some it was job loss and loss of self esteem combined with substance abuse. Three families (12%) reported job loss as a key factor in violence for the abuser. For another abuser it appeared to be on the job stress and job pressure. In three families (12%) any perceived loss of control over the female by the male resulted in violent behavior. Two female interviewees said their husbands were raised in families where violence was the way they dealt with frustration. One mother said she does not know what contributed to her husband's sexual abuse of their children

Alcohol or drug use

Fourteen families (20%) reported alcohol or drug use contributed to their becoming homeless; twelve were single-parent families. The substance use was primarily by the perpetrator of the domestic violence.

STRUGGLING TO SURVIVE

What families did to avoid losing housing

Twenty-nine families (43%) said they struggled to stay in their housing by a variety of means. Five sought legal help to no avail. Six families tried to negotiate with their landlord or relative for additional time. Seven families reported attempting to find jobs or additional jobs. Three families tried to get welfare assistance; four approached churches or other charitable organizations for help; and one borrowed money. Two families attempted to find less expensive housing, including making application for the Federal Section Eight Housing Program. (This program, administered through local Housing Authorities, allows qualified low-income families to pay thirty percent of their income for housing costs with the government paying the balance.)

Thirty-nine families (57%), said this question was not relevant for them because they left their housing voluntarily. Twenty-eight of these families (41%) moved out of their housing for what they saw as positive reasons: a new start, to find a job, or to better their lives. Eight of those families were actually fleeing abusive relationships. For eleven (16%) families, who also self-reported as voluntarily moving, the move from housing was regarded as negative but was not resisted because no alternative seemed feasible. Some of the families said they were being evicted by landlords, or "put out" by relatives or friends. Five single female heads of household reported they were left without funds by husbands, friends, or other relatives who moved out. Several families felt they were so far behind financially there was nothing they could do to catch up on rent payments so they "voluntarily" left.

Give or sell

Families gave up, sold, or lost some of their belongings in the process of becoming homeless. Thirty-four families (50%) sold things to raise money to stay in housing longer, pay other bills, or to be able to travel to Seattle. Twenty families (29%) claimed they had nothing of value to sell. Two single-female heads of households had everything stolen and sold by their boyfriends for drug money. Six families just left their property behind when they moved. Three evicted families had their belongings stolen off the sidewalk. Two families put things in storage and one family lost everything in a fire.

Tell relatives

Fourteen families (21%) did not tell their relatives or friends about their situation or potential loss of housing. This was either because they knew no help was available or, for a few families, because of embarrassment. Of the fifty two families (76%) who told their relatives or friends, twenty-four (46%) did receive some assistance. Help included emotional support, the offer to double-up or store things or a willingness to take some of the children temporarily. Twenty-four families (46%) did not receive help because their relatives or friends were in a similarly bad financial or health situation or just could not help.

What else was happening

When the families were asked what else was happening in their life at that time, twelve families (18%) could think of nothing in particular. The other fifty-six families (82%) experienced one or more significant and stressful life events prior to losing their housing. Ten families reported the loss of jobs, seven a death in the family, six an illness in the family, and five substance abuse. Four families had recently separated or divorced. Several women had recently had a baby, several others had spontaneously aborted a pregnancy, one woman twice in the last year. Several families describe having to split up their families and send some of the children away to live with relatives. Two families reported the involvement of Child Protective Services.

Last straw

Thirteen families (19%) considered the last event from which they could not recover and which caused them to become homeless was eviction. For twelve (18%) it was family problems, for seven (10%) it was job loss, for four (6%) battering or abuse, and for another four (6%) being around drug use and violence. Eight families (12%) claimed the last straw for them centered around money problems. Two families had their money stolen on their way to Seattle, two others ran out of money and "energy" during the move here. Some local residents could not pay their rent and could not find less expensive housing. A number of families were overwhelmed at being so in debt, "knowing that every cent we paid would not catch us up." For other families, special problems such as the death of a child or family member, the fire that burned everything, a house that was not ready to move into, living in a place that was substandard, or "seeing one's kids and everything falling apart" after a divorce, were considered the last straw. One mother summed up the ultimate obstacle for her, and unfortunately that of many others, when she said "despair".

Chapter V:

Effects of Homelessness

"We're not the same, not coping as well"

- a homeless family

HEALTH RELATED EFFECTS

Thirty-four families (50%) reported that one or more of their family members developed new physical health problems since becoming homeless. Other families claimed existing problems worsened. Colds, tiredness and generally not feeling well were the most frequent and common new problems.

Fifteen families (22%) said becoming homeless did not affect their mental or emotional health. (One might wonder if they were already so damaged, numb or steeled that adversity no longer phased them.) Fifty-two families (78%) reported that it had affected their families' mental or emotional health. For three families ending up in an emergency shelter was seen as both negative and positive. One family said the experience was making them stronger. They believed that "if you have faith in God you become stronger."

Depression in one or all of the family members was reported by forty-two (62%) of the homeless families. Additional families revealed that they "worry"; some are "angrier," "have problems with stress and fight more with [their] kids." A single mother reported that "it is overwhelming having to cope with so much, I feel like a basket case." A two parent family stated, "You're not the same anymore, it confuses you." Another claimed "we don't know what to expect" from day to day. One family described the emotional effects of being homeless and in a shelter as "mental anguish, [we] want to give up, [we] can't enjoy anything, everything gets on your nerves. Being here has really scared us — the drug dealing." A conscientious young father, an unemployed tradesman with a wife and baby, said he was, "frustrated and sometimes breaks down." He was also suffering from diabetes which he said affected his energy.

Where domestic violence had been a problem, the families were asked if becoming homeless resulted in an increase or decrease of child or spousal abuse in their family. Four families reported a decrease, one family an increase. Twelve families left their abuser. Two families said, for them, the question was not relevant since their abuser was currently in jail.

Eight (12%) families admitted an increase in alcohol or drug use since becoming homeless and attribute it to the additional stress incurred by being homeless. Thirty-nine families (59%) said there had been no change. Fourteen families (21%) reported a decrease, for some, because they left the user/abuser, and for three families because they had no money. Four families (6%) found the question not applicable because they were and had always been total abstainers.

CHILDREN AND FAMILY

Children and the move

Seventeen families (25%) reported that their children either did not know or were to young to know what was taking place when they became homeless. Fifty families (75%) had tried to explain the situation and what was going on to their children. The parents in forty-three families (63%) said they answered their children's questions as honestly and completely as they could. Four families (6%) reported they were not able to answer their children's questions, which may have indicated that the parents were as confused and unsure of what was going to happen as were their children.

Twenty-four families (48%) reported that their children were upset, shocked, or angry at becoming homeless. Eight families (16%) said their children accepted the move either with resignation or a willingness to do what was necessary. Fourteen families (28%) reported their children were glad to leave. Four families (8%) from out of state said the move was not a problem for their children, because the children liked to travel.

School age children

Forty-seven of the families (69%) in the shelters had a total of ninety school age children. Two children, not included in the above count, had already graduated from high school. Thirty-four of those families (72%) had their children enrolled in school. The other thirteen families (28%) did not. The majority of families (94%) whose children were enrolled in school also had them attending. The children of twenty-one families (66%) were attending the same school as they had before becoming homeless.

Thirteen families (41%) reported their children's school related behavior had been negatively affected since becoming homeless. Two children were repeating a grade; three were in jeopardy of being put back a year. Thirty families (64%) claimed the behavior of their children outside of school had also been affected.

The changes in behavior seen in the eleven to sixteen year old children were described as moodiness, resentment, trying to get away with things, becoming wild, picking up negative attitudes, more scatterbrained. One concerned mother reported her adolescent son was spending increasingly more time with downtown street kids. The behavior of some five to nine year old children was described as either rebellious, more daring, more disruptive, or "can't get along with nobody." For other children, the opposite behaviors were noticed; they were shy and insecure, needing to be with mom all the time, and without many friends.

Parents reported their children's activities were restricted
and different since they "can't do any extracurricular activities,"
were not around their friends, could not visit their friends, and did
not have access to a telephone. This last problem was cited by the
mother of two teenage girls. Some of the parents would not let
their children go outside to play because of drug abuse in the
neighborhood. According to her mother, one twelve year old girl
was required or "forced" by the situation to take on more
responsibility for her siblings.

Some changes in behavior were seen as beneficial. One
father described his four children as becoming more street wise,
more outgoing and able to mix and blend better. He saw these
changes as positive. The behavior of two eight and ten year old
brothers reportedly went "from wild to stable after moving here"
from a situation with even more insecurity and turmoil.

Preschool age children

Fifty families (73%) had a total of ninety-eight children
younger than school age. Thirty-five of those families (70%)
reported that the behavior of their small children changed since
becoming homeless. Twelve families said their young children
were more restless, hyperactive, not listening, rebellious, cranky,
aggressive, exhibiting "a mean attitude" and were harder to
handle. Some children were described as more withdrawn,
insecure, losing sleep and appetite, going back to diapers and
exhibiting a lot of sucking behavior. Other small children were
reported to be "acting strange and being sick" or just "knowing
something is wrong." Three families reported that their children
were troubled because they wanted to see their missing family
members. In describing her one year old, a mother said "it seems
like he worries and cries a lot." A six month old baby had a
permanent hoarse voice after being sick and living in a car for
weeks.

The daily activities of young children also changed since
moving into the shelter. Some mothers reported that they needed
to "drag" their children around on the bus with them. Others said

they did not have toys for their children and would not let their babies crawl on the floor with the roaches. A single mother, describing the behavior of her two and four year old children, said they "have grown up" since being there. One young family who had left an abusive situation reported that the children were now "not hitting other kids as much."

Caregiving responsibilities

The mother was the primary caregiver in fifty-four households (79%); in four families (6%), three of them headed by single males, the father was the primary caregiver. Eight families, thirty-nine percent of the two parent families, shared caregiving responsibilities equally between parents. Thirty-eight families (56%) said the difficulties of taking care of the family had increased since becoming homeless.

Acquiring food, getting adequate food and food storage was a problem mentioned by eleven families. Transportation, both to get food or supplies and to keep appointments, was a problem which made caregiving more difficult. Families reported that it was very difficult to stay clean. Families said, since they are out in the cold a lot, not having enough clothing was a problem. They needed to find shoes and warm clothes. Many families had zero income; every time the family needed soap, shampoo, toilet paper, disposable diapers, cleaning supplies or to wash clothes they first had to find money. Four families found that financially it was very hard to plan.

Parents said it was more difficult to take care of their children with no toys and no TV. With alcohol and drugs around, they felt they could not let their children go outside to play. Some parents found they were "yelling a lot more" at their children. Two families previously had house rules but since becoming homeless the rules had either had to be changed or dropped. A two-parent family reported, the "stress of everything" makes caregiving more difficult.

A single mother said it took "a lot of running around to get things done." Another parent reported there was "more responsibility, more to do." One two-parent family member thought it was "more difficult keeping things together." The mother in a two-parent family complained "I have so much on my mind, things are not normal, [I am] tired and emotionally beat." A two-parent family declared that often "you don't know where you will stay night to night"; a concerned parent said, "we don't know what's going to happen day to day." A single father with two young daughters reported "I need to make sure we have food and a place to stay." A divorced woman with four children complained "there's no time to do anything, job interviews interfere with picking kids up from school." On top of her own stress, a young mother worried that her mother with a bleeding ulcer might have to come live with them.

Two families, one of whom had been living in a car, felt relieved that they were in a shelter and their caregiving responsibilities had been made easier. At least while they were in the shelter, they had a place to stay and some food to eat.

Major effect on family

When the families described the major effect homelessness has made on their family, they frequently named stress and worry along with depression, feelings of insecurity, embarrassment, being degraded, hopelessness, and confusion. Some families reported increased arguing, bickering, and recurrent tears for both children and adults. Families said the experience changed their feelings toward each other. Some said feelings had gotten worse; two families had gotten closer.

Parents told of children worrying, some "being secretive," and others openly complaining, wanting their toys, wanting a telephone, wanting their own bed, or wanting to go home. A few parents told of trying to "put on a brave show" for their children.

Two families reported feelings of uncertainty, such as, not knowing where they were going to stay next or where they were going to get their next meal. One family reported that the major effect for them was being around people on drugs for the first time. Several families described unfortunate experiences at a previous shelter as the major effect of homelessness so far. One single father with two children said the hardest things for them were the little things, like trying to keep clothes clean and getting used to different beds.

Two families said they were shocked to realize that it really could happen to them and in seeing so many other families in the same homeless situation. One family said it made them appreciate what they had before. Several families said it made "everyone more determined to have a home," a "big old house." Seven families felt the major effect of becoming homeless for them was not being able to control their situation and having to give up regular activities; being broke, not having enough money to do the things they were once able to do, such as buying educational toys or games for their children or going out.

Job opportunities

The families were asked whether becoming homeless affected their employment or their job opportunities. Thirty families (44%) believed their employment and job opportunities had been negatively affected or had decreased since becoming homeless. Three families lost jobs since becoming homeless. Two families said a previous shelter made employment searches especially difficult since they were not allowed to use the shelter's address on job applications nor could they receive phone calls at the shelter or get phone messages. In order to work while living at that shelter, they needed a note from their employer to clock in or out of the shelter.

Nine families specifically mentioned the difficulty of trying to get a job without their own phone or a permanent address. One employed father had lost extra work because of not being reachable by phone when the employer needed him. Job searches proved very difficult for another family after using up their allotted bus tokens. Three families from out of state felt that not having local references would make obtaining a job more difficult. One single father with four children said being homeless was "harder in the area of childcare," since he had "to leave the kids by themselves." Two families reported that, when homeless, you "don't have time to do it all" and you "give up easier."

Twenty-one families (31%) said they had experienced no change in potential employment opportunities since becoming homeless. For five families, medical problems were the primary hindrance. Twelve families (18%) said either they did not know if their job opportunities would be affected or the question was not applicable to them. Five families (7%) thought their employment opportunities had been increased. Two families had recently gotten jobs, one woman as a chore service worker based specifically on her special need and homeless situation.

Would you work?

Fifty-five families (81%) said they would take a job if one became available; four families (6%) reported they would not take a job at that time. Of those four, one family could not take a job for medical reasons. A single father felt his children needed his supervision; one mother wanted to take care of her handicapped daughter; and one young woman wanted to go to school. Four families (6%) said they would accept the job only if certain conditions were met. Five other females (7%), who said they would decline the hypothetical job, already had spouses working and wanted to stay home to take care of their young children.

Twenty families (29%) reported no reason they would not work. Twenty-one families (31%) declared they would not work if there was no childcare. Eight families (12%) said they would not take a job if the pay is too low; six families (9%) said they could not take a job until they completed medical treatments. Two single women did not think a job was realistic for them at that time because they were pregnant and their regular kind of work was too strenuous. Two young women heads of household, wanted further job training, one by continuing a program already started through the Division of Vocational Rehabilitation.

Chapter VI:

Family Recommendations

"Provide counseling for whatever problems they have."
- unemployed family from Oregon

PREVENTING FAMILY HOMELESSNESS

Most helpful

The families each had their own opinion of what would have been most helpful to prevent them from becoming homeless. The single most important thing, fifteen families (22%) said they needed, was low-income housing. Seven families (10%), who had voluntarily relocated, thought either they should not have moved or should have planned it better and had more money. Four families (6%) said assistance with rent or utility payments would have been most helpful for them. Better laws or restraining orders on their batterers would have helped three families (4%). Not being cut off from welfare or disability benefits would have helped four families (6%). Many families offered one of a kind suggestions for what would have helped to prevent their homelessness, such as, not having a wife end up in the hospital, not putting money where it could be stolen, a stronger labor union, a better landlord, or managing money differently. One family suggested an all-inclusive measure that would have prevented them from becoming homeless and one which would have averted it for most of the families. That was, "not being vulnerable and having things happen."

In taking advantage of the opportunity to make recommendations for programs that would prevent families from becoming homeless, many families made multiple suggestions. A recommendation repeated several times was that there be education about the things that cause homelessness. Several families suggested that there were already programs in existence that might have prevented them from becoming homeless had they known about them. The families strongly suggested that these programs be publicized. One family claimed that "welfare doesn't tell you anything about housing." The families that had no knowledge of such programs, said the first thing government should do is to "put a thirty minute program on television telling what is available to the public in the way of help."

Housing concerns

The majority of recommendations for programs dealt specifically with housing issues. Twenty families requested additional housing, and nine families, more low-income, or Section Eight housing, specifically. Eleven families suggested changes in the private sector rental market, where most of the families had previously been housed. A need was expressed for:

- lower rents or rental assistance for low-income people
- providing emergency rental grants or financial aid to pay rent and help with deposits
- "more suitable places for families to live, not like projects," "larger places with bigger rooms," "more livable apartments that allowed pets without an extra charge"
- stricter rules for landlords
- a clause that requires and insures that apartment managers can't evict people on welfare but must work with them
- having the government take over the house mortgage for homeowners experiencing financial difficulty and have the family make payments to them

- an agency where you could find affordable housing such as fixer-ups
- low-income or subsidized housing made available automatically
- more liberal guidelines for getting into housing
- being able to bump others from low-income housing
- a one year time limit on Section Eight housing to allow others access

Employment issues

The families made the next largest number of recommendations concerning employment issues. Thirteen families suggested the creation of more jobs; seven suggested job training. Seven families recommended more affordable daycare for children. Other suggestions related to employment issues consisted of:

- better job training, quicker employment service
- more work programs
- on the job training with pay while learning
- assistance in getting jobs that support families
- a program that teaches job skills and money management together
- counseling, if the homeless can't find a job
- have government give the applicant a questionnaire for employers to fill out regarding why the applicant was not hired
- medical welfare assistance for working families

Welfare assistance

Fifteen families made suggestions regarding welfare assistance. They recommend that government:

- have less "red tape" to get on welfare

- make sure every family gets an allotment check
- provide a larger welfare check
- give welfare but make recipients work so it's not just a handout
- send rent payment directly to landlord
- help welfare recipient once a month with a plan to pay bills
- help welfare recipients plan to shop for healthy food
- give checks twice a month instead of all the money at the beginning of the month
- put food stamps on a credit card so they can't be sold
- have a system to check on welfare cheats
- have liaison between welfare and other government programs to ensure that they work together for the good of the client

To sensitize public officials to the needs of the homeless, families recommended that public officials come see what it is like and talk to the people about their problems. They said the government should put more emphasis on the homeless here instead of abroad. "Give our own people $2500, like the boat people." (Boat people refers to refugees that escaped from Vietnam by boat and are being helped to resettle in this country.)

General measures the families suggested to prevent other families from becoming homeless were that there be:

- legal aid available
- stiffer penalties for violence and abuse
- counseling on whatever problems they have
- motivation counseling or classes
- money management classes
- help with budgeting
- workers that care about people
- careful interviews about drug use

Most important problem

After making recommendations for a program to prevent homelessness, the families gave their opinion on which one problem was the most important to address. Thirty-six families (55%) suggested housing, nine families (12%) said more jobs or higher minimum wage, and three families (5%) said drug and alcohol counseling. Eighteen families (28%) had other ideas as to what they thought was most important. They included:

- guaranteeing food and shelter for children
- letting people know about the programs available and how to access them
- help with food, dental, medical, and welfare assistance
- help for violence, "it has a lot of emotional effects"
- counseling for men who beat up on women and children
- anything to help a family from losing their home
- financial assistance for rent and expenses
- the first large payment needed to move into a place
- help people stand on their own and support themselves

ASSISTING HOMELESS FAMILIES

Most needed

The families were asked what would help them most to get back into secure, stable housing. Thirty-four families (50%) said more housing is necessary, twelve replied with just the word "housing" and eleven specified Section Eight or low-income housing. Twenty-one families (31%) thought what would help them most was a good job. Thirteen families (19%) said for them, more money or higher benefits. One family believed that job training would be most helpful for them.

Counseling

The parents were asked if they or their children needed or would benefit by counseling to help overcome or deal with problems related to being homeless. Twenty-five families (37%) said they did not need counseling. Thirty-three adults (50%) reported that they needed or would benefit by counseling. Eight adults (12%) said maybe they would benefit by counseling. Twenty-four (43%) families thought one or more of their children needed or would benefit by counseling and seven families (12%) thought maybe their children would benefit by counseling.

The families were asked what kinds of counseling they would find helpful. Twenty-eight families wanted counseling for emotional problems. Eight believed family counseling would help. Nine families thought drug or alcohol counseling would be helpful. Twenty-three families wanted employment counseling and twenty-seven wanted financial counseling. Seventeen families thought their school children needed or would benefit by school counseling or tutoring. Thirty-four families wanted or thought they could use counseling related to housing. Six families believed there might be other kinds of counseling from which they would benefit.

Program components

As the final question, the families were asked to give ideas for programs designed to help families that were already homeless. Some responses were similar to those given for what should be done to prevent families from becoming homeless. They said the government should:

- "Put more money in the right place; too much is on military"
- help with jobs, give "help for people in America"
- provide food, shelter and medical help

Shelters

Sixteen families recommended more emergency shelters for homeless families. Other suggestions were to:

- go around and pick up homeless families with kids
- increase the staff at the shelters
- make all family shelters easier to get into (without a marriage license or birth certificate)
- have residents work at the shelter in order to stay, "so they retain dignity"
- have a place for older kids to meet and do things
- recreation to relieve stress
- have a community room where people can be together;
- "they tend to isolate themselves in depression"
- allow longer stays in shelters
- have long-term shelter where families can work off part of the rent
- get the homeless money for food and clothing
- make sanitary standards higher in shelters
- clean up shelter apartments, clean up drugs
- more supervision
- close [intense] counseling while in shelter

Interim housing

As a necessary step between emergency shelter and housing, several program suggestions were made:

- family shelters should have some kind of interim housing program
- six month transitional housing to save up money - have counselors help
- interim housing for six months so they can get into low income housing

Low-income housing

Eleven families suggested more low-income housing to help families that are homeless; three suggested housing set-asides for homeless families. Twenty-six additional housing-related recommendations designed to help families already homeless included:

- don't build bombs, build more low-income housing
- fund shelters and housing for families
- check for those needing just a place to stay
- use homes sitting vacant
- use buildings with empty spaces
- take vacant building downtown and fix up for homeless
- help with money to get into a permanent place
- if people are homeless for legitimate reasons get them into housing quickly
- help with ground work needed to get into housing
- help in finding a place or give extensions in shelter if they haven't money or places to look for rentals
- help to get into Section Eight housing more quickly
- more housing for expectant parents
- help to get into low-income housing faster
- make it easier to get public housing, especially important for those from out of state
- help to get into apartments, like Salvation Army
- waiting lists (for housing) are too long, need a separate list for those in emergency need
- give more information to apartment owners on Section Eight certificates and vouchers
- send rent payment directly to landlord
- provide landlord tenant negotiations
- encourage rent pledges
- affordable housing for low-income families
- places to upgrade standard of living
- better neighborhoods where there are no drugs and people are more positive
- people should get together, get funds to get a place

Childcare

Seven families recommended more childcare programs. Additional suggestions were for childcare, both while looking for a job and after.

Jobs

Eight families advocated providing more jobs. Five families proposed education or training to get jobs. Other employment-related suggestions for families were:

- teach homeless families to become farmers
- give people jobs; employment is needed to regain pride
- a work program for mothers with small children
- help finding work
- jobs for adults or teens on a bus line if they have no transportation
- more jobs for the men
- separate employment division for immediate jobs
- jobs set aside for homeless till they could move on
- run work programs out of shelter and welfare office

Counseling

Six families requested making counseling available to homeless families, group counseling, family counseling, counseling on how to handle money and counseling on how to cope, how not to be dysfunctional. Related suggestions were:

- find out why they are homeless, help with those problems
- sit down and talk to them, make them aware of the programs available
- provide motivational training, role models

- alcohol and drug programs for homeless
- provide feelings of security with help in setting and reaching goals
- develop a good general program with a support group
- motivation classes to give boost and objectives
- something to help people better themselves
- someone to tell where to turn, how to manage
- teach them to live the best they can until they can do better

Welfare

Regarding financial assistance programs or welfare, the families recommended:

- funding for emergency need
- a fund to help people get started, a loan to pay back
- a decent amount of money with a way to work it off and feel like we are earning it
- contacting agencies to help with utility needs, etc.
- make sure every family gets an allotment check
- put food stamps on credit cards so can't be sold

Seven families were so overwhelmed by their own homelessness that they were at a loss for ideas on what to include in a program designed to deal with the problem.

Chapter VII:

Discussion

A NEW TYPOLOGY

As the study was being completed and the data were analyzed a new and kaleidoscopic picture of the homeless family was seen. The image was continuously being changed and influenced by the variety of ways they reported becoming homeless. It was found that not all homeless families were forced out of their housing; over half, fifty-seven percent, say they left voluntarily. This unexpected and surprising revelation led to a further examination of the data, and a new typology of homeless families began to appear. It was discovered that in addition to the obvious and well documented cases of flight from domestic violence, there are other situations felt to be so onerous or dangerous that just getting away, removing one's family, seems to be the best or only alternative to staying. The most common single reason families give for leaving their home and familiar surroundings, is the same motivation generally accepted and practiced by many middle class families. That is, to undertake a geographic move with one's children, in tow, for new or better employment opportunities.

As tentative categories in the new typology, the families who fall into the three clusters described above are thought of and termed "Improvers" because that is their stated purpose for voluntarily leaving their homes or housing. Some families report that they actually prepared for their move by doing research on cities and their laws, selling belongings to get money together, and by locating places to stay on the way or when they got here, usually with relatives or friends. But others, also meeting the Improver classification definition, seem to move from their housing more as a reaction to aversive situations and seemingly without much forethought or planning. (These characteristics suggested possible further categorical differentiation.)

It was soon determined that some families, who initially claimed to have left their housing voluntarily, actually moved out because they received eviction notices. Others believed they were so in debt, eviction was imminent so they left before it occured. Some families, who reported leaving voluntarily, had been ordered out or abandoned by relatives or friends with whom they were doubled-up. Becoming homeless in these ways was seen as the result of events that seemed to befall a family just trying to hang on to what they had. These were situations over which they felt they had no control. In the typology these families were referred to as "Maintainers" because families were seen as trying to keep things together, to maintain the status quo. The typical categorical events, initiated by others, that result in such families becoming homeless, are found to be eviction, rejection by friends or relatives and abandonment by spouse, relatives or friends. The families' reactions vary from accepting to resisting.

The typology of homeless families and a definitional outline was formulated by using the initiating or non initiating behavior, in response to financial, housing or relationship problems, as the determinant of Improver or Maintainer categories. The various categories were envisioned as points along a continuum; however, for purposes of illustration, they will be interpreted and treated as dichotomous in a tentative way. The cases falling near the center of the continuum were seen as having many similarities.

The definitional outline also indicates some tentative sub-categories delineating differences in the stated behaviors and motivation precipitating the families' homeless condition. It is acknowledged that some of the differences in behavior and coping style may be due in part to the varing amounts of adversity the families were facing at the time and their perception, realistic or not, of the options open to them.

As an exercise to further test and explore the typology, all families interviewed were classified according to the above schemata. The primary decision for which category they fell into was determined by response to their answers to the question, "What did you do to keep from losing your housing?" It was found that sometimes a family's behavioral category appeared to change when answers to later questions were reviewed, such as an Improver family later being rejected by relatives. The family was kept in the earlier primary category because of their initial motivation for first leaving housing. Based on the cases falling into these tentative categories, further analysis was undertaken to ascertain whether other differences in population characteristics would show up in the answers to additional questions.

This population sample split evenly into thirty-four Improver families and thirty-four Maintainer families. The Improvers consist of eighteen single parent families and sixteen two parent families; and the Maintainers, nineteen single parent families and fifteen two parent families. The population from the two shelters falls fairly equally into the Improver and Maintainer groups. Case examples from families in the sample are used to illustrate the various primary Improver and Maintainer categories. (See chapter 8.)

INITIATING

Improvers (instigate a move to better their lives)
    Workers (move geographically to find work)
        [Planners (research and prepare for move)]
        [Reactors (leave in a hurry without planning)]
    Defenders (move to safeguard children)
        [Planners (research and prepare for move)]
        [Reactors (leave in a hurry without planning)]
    Escapers (flee from domestic violence)
        [Planners (research and prepare for move)]
        [Reactors (leave in a hurry without planning)]

NON-INITIATING

Maintainers (events they could not control took over)
    Evicted (evicted by landlord or relatives)
        [Acquiescers (accept move with resignation)]
        [Fighters (try to get help or reprieve)]
    Rejected (told by relatives or friends to leave)
        [Acquiescers (accept move with resignation)]
        [Fighters (try to negotiate, get reprieve)]
    Abandoned (relatives or friends left, moved away)
        [Acquiescers (accept move with resignation)]
        [Fighters (try to get help or reprieve)]

Figure 1. Definitional Outline of Typology

IMPROVERS					
n = 34 (50%)					
Workers = 18		Defenders = 8		Escapers = 8	
planner	reactor	planner	reactor	planner	reactor
4	14	2	6	4	4

single parent families = 18
two parent families = 16

MAINTAINERS					
n = 34 (50%)					
Evicted = 21		Rejected = 8		Abandoned = 5	
planner	reactor	planner	reactor	planner	reactor
7	14	5	3	4	1

Single-parent families	= 19
Two-parent families	= 15
Total families	= 68

Figure 2. Families classified by behaviors

SILHOUETTES

A further analysis indicates that the families falling into the major categories of Improver and Maintainer have some measureable and possibly significant differences.

Households

The types of parental households in each group is approximately the same. Improver group families contains eighteen single parent households, two of them headed by single males, and sixteen two parent families. The Maintainer family group is composed of nineteen single parent households, one of them male headed, and sixteen two parent families. The Improver families have fifty adults and total of seventy-seven children. The number of children per family ranges from one to four and averages two per family. They have a total of forty-nine adults and one hundred and thirteen children. The number of children per family ranges from one to seven with an average of three per family, the same as the sample as a whole. Although the number of adults in each group is nearly the same, the fact that there are more children in Maintainer families may negatively influence their willingness and ability to move.

Age comparisons

The average ages of the adults of the two groups differ by one year for the females and by four years for the males. The ages of the Improver adults range from eighteen to forty-nine, with a mean age of twenty-nine years old for both females and males. The forty-nine year old grandmother is head of household for her Improver group family. The seventy-seven (40%) Improver family children range in age from less than one year to seventeen. In the Maintainer group, the parent's ages range from twenty to forty-seven, with the mean age of females, twenty-eight, and males, thirty-three. Maintainer children range in age from less than one year to nineteen.

Ethnic comparisons

The Improver category families contain fifty adults, twenty-five (50%) of them white, seventeen (34%) black, four (8%) Latino, and four (8%) Native American. The Maintainer category families have forty-nine adults, twenty-one (43%) white, twenty-three (47%) black, one (2%) Latino, two (4%) Native American and two (4%) Hawaiian.

A comparison of the two groups shows variation in racial composition but the disparity is even more pronounced when the adult females are looked at separately. The Improver group had eighteen white females (56%) and ten black females (31%), while the Maintainer group's situation was practically the reverse, with eighteen black females (54%) and twelve white females (36%). The fact that more Maintainer females (63%) were from minority races may reflect some subtle effects of racial prejudice. Experiencing society's prejudice might have affected the minority female's belief that she could get away from or overcome her problems through her own efforts and thus prevented her from trying.

Education

With a high school education considered the common denominator, the groups can be judged roughly equivalent in formal education. One person in each group had a master's degree.

Table 5. Demographics of Improver and Maintainer Families

	Improver		Maintainer	
No of adults	50		51	
Ages of females	18-49	mn29	20-37	mn28
Ages of males	19-45	mn29	25-47	mn33
Children	77		113	
Average # children	2	(1-4)	3	(1-7)
Single-parent families	18		19	
Two-parent families	16		15	

Ethnicity (all adults)	Improver		Maintainer	
Caucasian	25	(50%)	21	(43%)
African-American	17	(34%)	23	(47%)
Other	8	(16%)	5	(10%)

Ethnicity (all females)	Improver		Maintainer	
Caucasian	18	(56%)	12	(36%)
African-American	10	(31%)	18	(54%)
Other	4	(12%)	3	(9%)

Geographic origin

As might be expected, more families from the Improver group than the Maintainer group are from out of state. In the Improver group, ten families are Washington State residents; twenty-four came from other states. Twenty-one of those lived only in Washington State since becoming homeless; they were not homeless before they left their previous area but became so after their resources proved insufficient when they got here. Eleven Improver group families came here after becoming homeless elsewhere. In the Maintainer group, five families were from out of state and twenty-nine were state residents. Twenty-eight lived only in Washington since becoming homeless, seven families came or returned to Seattle after they became homeless.

Their reasons for coming here show that the move was not made randomly. Even when moving for a job or to get away from domestic violence, picking an area where one has relatives or has lived previously makes the transition easier and increases the likelihood of success. We found that seven families in the Improver group moved to Seattle because they had family in the area, seven because they were looking for or had been promised a job, and six were former residents. Four families moved to get away from an abuser, and two for other reasons.

Five families in the Maintainer group said they moved to Seattle because they had relatives in the area, two were looking for a job, one family had lived here previously, and six reportedly moved for other reasons, including the family with the difficult pregnancy. The Maintainers spent more time after losing housing doubled up with relatives and had been homeless for the most protracted length of time. Two Maintainer families had actually been homeless for two and a half to three years.

Income

Before becoming homeless, the monthly income of the Improver families ranged from $0 to $4200; the mean was $1255. Eighteen Improver families (53%) received all of their income from employment and six from a combination of employment and government grants. Seven were receiving their income from AFDC grants. The Maintainer monthly incomes before becoming homeless ranged from $0 to $2800, with a mean of $897.47. Thirteen Maintainer families obtained their income from employment, two from a combination of employment and grants, and twelve from AFDC.

Twenty-five (74%) of the Improver families with higher average incomes, were able to keep up with their bills and nine (26%) were not. Fourteen (41%) Maintainer families say they were able to pay their bills and nineteen (56%) say they were not. As might be expected, because of their lower income, more Maintainer families used government assistant programs, food banks, and utility assistance than Improver families.

The Improver families with a higher average income probably had higher expectations when they left their housing to look for a job or to improve their personal situation. Their loss of income was found to be greater and more complete than for Maintainer families because more Improver families had been employed and were depending on finding jobs for income. They did not have the backup of government grants in place to support them when they could not find employment.

The Improver families report the most drastic change in income, ranging from $0 to $800 dollars with a mean of $267.22, down $988, to only twenty-one percent of their average previous income. Seven families still get their income from AFDC but only four receive all their income from employment and only one from a combination of employment and government program. Nineteen Improver families report no current income.

The Maintainers report present income ranging from $0 to $1100 with a mean of $519.50, down $378, fifty-eight of what they had before. Nine families receive all their income from employment and fifteen from AFDC. Seven Maintainer families say they have no present income.

Kind of work

As their regular kind of work, thirteen Improver females report service jobs; three professional jobs; three, manual jobs; four, clerical jobs; and two, technical jobs. Maintainer females report sixteen service jobs, one professional, one manual, and two technical jobs. Four Improver and seven Maintainer females stayed home as full time homemakers prior to becoming homeless. Four Maintainer females were employed. No Improver female was employed at the time of interview. The Improver and Maintainer males were represented fairly equitably in the variety of jobs held by the males. The two groups had used childcare with equal frequency.

Problem comparison

Differences already pointed out in the typological categories give clues to the problems the families cite as contributing to their homelessness. A variation in ranking order is primarily what we notice for the first problem. The Improver families list no job, followed by no money, domestic violence, substance abuse, lack of low-income housing, and other unique problems as the most significant factors contributing to their loss of housing. The Maintainer families give equal rating to no money and no job followed by substance abuse, domestic violence and other unique problems.

Improver families cite no money or financial problems most frequently as their secondary problem, followed by no job, substance abuse, domestic violence, and again no low-income housing. The Maintainer families rate lack of job followed by eviction, financial problems, and no money as their secondary problem. The factors cited begins to differentiate the two groups in the answers to this question. Improver families indicate substance abuse, domestic violence, and lack of low-income housing as their second problem with the same frequency as Maintainer families are citing eviction. For their tertiary problem,

Improver families again include domestic violence and substance abuse while Maintainer families cite eviction.

Health problems do not appear to be a significant factor separating the Improver group families from the Maintainers. One more Maintainer family reports physical health problems before losing housing than do Improver families. But, four Improver families claim more than one member of their family had health problems in contrast to one Maintainer family.

Stress and depression before becoming homeless also are found to be roughly equivalent in each group. Domestic violence is more commonly given as a cause of stress for families in the Improver group. Financial concerns and threatened eviction are more prevalent as causes of Maintainer stress.

Six of the ten families citing divorce as a contributing to homelessness are in the Improver group. As one might expect from answers to earlier questions, domestic violence is more frequently reported as a problem for Improver families. Ten Improver and six Maintainer families say domestic violence was the reason they sought shelter. One family from each group said it was partly the reason. Although fewer Maintainer families report domestic violence, no Maintainer family reporting abuse described it as lasting for less than two years. The effect of being abused over longer periods of time may have contributed to a loss of self confidence in their ability to move out in an attempt to better their lives.

Eight Improver families and five Maintainers say alcohol or drug use caused increased violence. Three Maintainer families report job loss as a key factor in violence. In three Improver families, a percieved loss of control over the famale resulted in violent behavior by the male. Ten Improver and four Maintainer families report alcohol or drug use contributed to their becoming homeless.

Fighting Homelessness

Five Improver families say they tried to get jobs or additional jobs to avoid homelessness. Equal numbers of both groups told their relatives or friends and equal numbers reported getting some help from them. Eight Maintainer and four Improver families report nothing else noteworthy was going on in their lives. The others had additional problems to deal with.

The last straw for the Improver families centers around loss of or lack of jobs, running out of money, battering or abuse and family problems. Maintainers report their last straw was primarily eviction and family problems including being pushed out by family members.

Children

More Maintainer children were upset about the move from housing; more Improver children were glad to leave and reportedly liked to travel, but the differences were small.

The number of families with school age children was greater for the Maintainer group but the percentages of families in each group with children enrolled and attending were approximately the same. The Maintainer families had more children attending the same school as they did before becoming homeless. The parents report the school behavior of more Improver children (53%) than Maintainer children (29%) was negatively affected. This might be explained, in part, by the fact that more of them had to change schools

The behavior and activity changes reported for the younger children were seen as similar in both groups. Homelessness seems to be a great leveler.

As discussed earlier, many Improver families moved from their previous housing to find jobs. They continue to express more eagerness than Maintainers to accept jobs with few stipulations except the availability of childcare. Except for those with complicated circumstances, the Improver families in general thought they could be back into regular housing in a shorter period of time than Maintainers families.

Family advice

The recommendations and suggestions made for programs to prevent homelessness appeared to differientiate and reflect the behaviorial classification and coping style of the families. Families that fell into the Improver categories mentioned the need for employment frequently, but only slightly more than the need for more housing. The Maintainers, who had essentially been pushed out of housing, voiced a need for more affordable housing almost twice as often as job related concerns. The same trends are seen in the measures and programs recommended to assist families already homeless. Maintainers were three times more likely to suggest increased availability to low-income housing as they were to give employment related suggestions. The Improvers express nearly equal concern about access to jobs as to housing. Both the Maintainers and Improver category families are evenly represented in the recommendation that emergency shelters be an essential part of a program to assist homeless families and that counseling be included in the program to rehabilitate both the parents and their children.

Chapter VIII:

The Kaleidoscopic Picture

As we see families becoming homelessness in different ways the image of the homeless family changes and gives evidence of a possible new typology. To illustrate the categories discussed in the previous chapter case examples from families in the sample are described. The names of the families have been changed.

THE IMPROVERS

Thirty-four of the families (51%) left their housing voluntarily with the intention and goal of bettering their lives or the lives of their children; these are the Improvers.

Workers

Eighteen Improver families (26%) were further classified as Workers and fifteen of those were found to be two parent families. These families left their previous housing after they lost employment and felt they had exhausted the job possibilities in their local area. They later became homeless as a result of inadequate planning, mishaps or hoped for jobs that either didn't materialize or fell through.

The Smith family is a Worker family who
moved from Virginia for a job. The Smith family
consists of a mother, father and a four year old child.
Mr. Smith's regular employment was in carpentry
and Mrs. Smith worked as a cocktail waitress. When
employed, they had a combined monthly income of
approximately $1300. It was six months since the
family had steady employment and Mr. Smith was
drawing workman's compensation. When the family
heard that Mr. Smith had a job waiting in Seattle, they
voluntarily sold their furniture and other belongings
in order to move.

After arriving in Seattle they found out that the
job had fallen through. Without money or a job they
quickly became homeless. This family is staying in a
shelter and is very depressed. Mrs. Smith reports that
the major effect of homelessness on their family is
reflected in their attitudes. Caregiving is more
difficult, they "have grown apart and love toward
each other is not there." The four year old boy "is
hard to get along with, is aggressive and has a mean
attitude." The use of alcohol or drugs has increased
for the adults.

Defenders

Nine of the single-parent Improver families fit the definition
of Defenders. These families were living in environments which
they considered dangerous. They left their housing because of the
drug abuse, violence and crime in their immediate vicinity. These
single parent families said they moved in order to protect the lives,
well being and future of their children. They wanted to start over
in a new area.

The Roberts family is an example of a Defender
family. Mrs. Roberts has two daughters, ages six and
eight. They left their housing in California because

Mrs. Roberts wanted to get her daughters away from the environment they were living in – of drugs, guns, and crime. The children's grandmother agreed with Mrs. Roberts that the move was a good idea even though she would miss seeing the girls. Mrs. Roberts said they did not originally plan to come to stay in Seattle but when driving through they "kind of liked it"; the girls liked the snow.

Mrs. Robert's regular kind of work is either as a waitress or in cosmetology but she has not worked for about two years and she and the girls were on AFDC. Although still married, Mr. Roberts was not with them. His regular kind of work was as a contractor but he hadn't worked in four to five months. When asked if becoming homeless had affected their health the young mother said she "doesn't eat much, has lost a lot of weight and has had two miscarriages in the last year but the girls are fine." Mrs. Roberts weighed about eighty pounds. Her six year old daughter has had to repeat a grade since becoming homeless. The family gave up most of their belongings in order to move.

Escapers

The Escapers have some similarities to both the Workers and the Defenders, because they also took the initiative to move away from "home". These families, nine of them in this sample, are single-female headed households. They said they left abusive relationships for their own survival or that of their children.

The Peters family is an example of an Escaper family. Mrs. Peters is a divorced, twenty-eight year old mother of three children from Pennsylvania. To support his drug habit, Mr. Peters stole from the family and from his wife's restaurant business until it went bankrupt. When using drugs, alcohol or

sniffing glue, Mr. Peters would become very violent,
threaten and beat up his wife. He would get drunk,
then take the baby away, which terrified Mrs. Peters.
After three years of abuse Mrs. Peters ended up in the
hospital with a fractured skull. Before Mr. Peters
could inflict any more physical or emotional damage,
Mrs. Peters filed criminal charges and started divorce
proceedings. With a bankrupt business and no credit
available, Mrs. Peters borrowed a credit card from
her mother and flew to Seattle where her mother
lives.

Her nine year old son is currently living with
relatives in another state; his grades have dropped and
he is in counseling. The five year old, middle child is
autistic and not presently in school. She will have to
start her special education program over. The baby,
now two years old, says he wants to see his daddy.
Mrs. Peters claims that the major effect of becoming
homeless, experienced by her family, is that of
"insecurity, everything changing, and no sense of
belonging."

Unfortunately whether the Improvers, Defenders, or
Escapers planned and gathered their resources for the move, or
not, the resources they mustered were not sufficient to provide
them entry into new housing or the job market. One Escaper
family leaving an abusive situation reportedly found out by
researching the problem that Washington State was one of the
better states for the protection of women's rights. Although this
woman's financial resources did not provide her family housing
when they arrived, she felt the benefits of her research and
planning were not in vain.

THE MAINTAINERS

In contrast to the homeless families who left their housing voluntarily because they chose to move to improve their lives or escape abuse, another major classification of homeless families may be called the Maintainers. The thirty three families who fell into this category made up forty-nine percent of the population surveyed. These families were living and surviving in their housing as well as they could when events they could not seem to control took over and they lost their housing.

Maintainers are divided into three sub-categories, those who were Evicted from housing by a landlord, those who were ordered out or Rejected by the friends or relatives with whom they were doubled-up and those who were Abandoned and left behind when the spouses, friends, or relatives with whom they were living moved away.

As with the Improver categories, there is some evidence that there may be further refinement of the Maintainer sub-categories possible. It is based on the reported coping style of the family; how they reacted to their threatened loss of housing. Those who acquiesced and accepted the move reportedly believed they had no other options. They felt powerless; either they were in the wrong or, if not, there was no recourse available. Those who fought to keep their housing resisted because they thought they were being unjustly treated and the situation or the landlord was unreasonable or unfair.

Evicted

The tentative categories of Acquiescers and Fighters will be briefly explored in the Evicted category.

The Browns are a two-parent family with three children that fit the tentative Evicted-acquiescer category. Mr. Brown was laid off from his $1900 per month job at the shipyards as a welder but Mrs.

Brown was able to keep her $800 per month employment doing data entry. As Mr. Brown's unemployment continued he "did other little jobs" to come up with the rent but bill problems developed and the family pushed its credit purchases up to the limit. Fearing that Mrs. Brown's wages would be garnished because of more debt, they moved from their apartment to the shelter. The Brown's sold their car and TV to pay for food, necessities and storage of their other belongings.

They answered their children's questions about what was happening "as well as they could" and the oldest, a ten year old, seemed to understand. Mr. Brown feels a great deal of frustration at being unemployed and not being able to provide for his family. He reports that the last straw that caused them to become homeless was "not being a financially responsible person with the money that I had". Mr. Brown reports that everybody in the family is more depressed. The major effect of homelessness on his family is "being deprived"; he says it is "degrading". Mr. Brown suggests that a program to help homeless families include daycare so the unemployed parents can look for work.

The Thomases are an example of an Evicted single parent family that tried to resist. Ms. Thomas has three sons aged nine, twelve and fifteen. Ms. Thomas was barely able to support her family with food stamps and her $500 per month job as a cosmetologist when her mother, who lived nearby, developed cancer and became bedridden. Ms. Thomas could not take her mother into her apartment but agreed to share the caretaking responsibilities with her sisters. In addition to providing care for her own children, Ms. Thomas spent time before work, during lunch hour and after work taking care of her mother, cooking, bathing and reading to her. Ms. Thomas recounted that "It took a lot of energy."

The beauty shop owner was very accommodating to Ms. Thomas and the time spent away, but of course had to pay according to the time worked. As bills mounted Ms. Thomas went to the welfare department for help. She was told she was not eligible because she had a job. Ms. Thomas ultimately was forced to quit her job to take care of her dying mother.

After her mother's death she became depressed and "felt alone with her problems." She reported she "didn't care about things much at that time." Although she went back to work they were not able to pay bills and she told her sons they would have to go to a shelter. They were upset but she told them the choices were "do it [go to a shelter], live on a park bench or be split up in foster care." Ms. Thomas said she did not tell her relatives or friends about losing her housing because she didn't think they could help anyway and didn't want to put them on the spot. She considers the final straw that caused them to become homeless was not being able to get help from welfare or from the housing authority.

The first shelter they went to was a very distressing experience for the family and made them doubly depressed. Ms. Thomas felt looked down on and treated like a child and "they didn't know how to treat children." This shelter required that they clock in and out and required a note from the employer to work. The family eventually left this shelter when one of the sons was refused entrance to the shelter after an athletic program he participated in went later than expected. The coach accompanied the boy to explain the delay but to no avail.

Ms. Thomas feels strongly that the whole family needs counseling. She is angry and said "you become hard and protective of your things and got to undo some thinking." "Its their fault that I am homeless. I am going to ask them for all I can. They wouldn't give to me when I needed only a little." She wants her sons to know "being homeless is not shameful, not using the resources available is wrong." Ms. Thomas is on leave from her job and now receives $500 per month from AFDC. She said she will work but needs to take care of her kids first.

Rejected

These are families that have experienced an inability to provide for or maintain housing for their family so they double-up temporarily with relatives or friends, hopefully until their situation improves. Rather than solving their problems, the doubling-up creates new ones for both families and they are rejected and asked to leave.

Miss Barber is a twenty-two year old young woman, the mother of five month old twins; she fits the category of Rejected. She and her boyfriend were living with her grandmother while she was pregnant. When her grandmother died, her uncle "put her out". The father of the babies was no help; they were always arguing and "he would sometimes slap or hit me." Her boyfriend abused her off and on for five years. Miss Barber went to stay with her aunt until the babies were born, then she had to move on. She heard that they helped homeless families more in Seattle so she moved up here with her mother and two babies. She tries not to get depressed, by reading the Bible, and talking to her mother. She says "I can't be weak." She said now that she is in the shelter, the babies have colds, cry more and want her to pick them up all the time. She worked two years ago as a cashier and will work again if she can get child care.

Abandoned

The Rejected and the Abandoned have many similarities. They are living with relatives or with friends and depend on that relationship and living condition to either survive or to tide them over until they can find a way to make it on their own. The Rejected are pushed out of their temporary housing situation before they are ready and the Abandoned are left in the housing but without the financial means to pay for it. Abandoned wives or husbands fit this latter category as do families living with a relative or friend who decides that the situation is too difficult and just leaves.

Mrs. Jones is an example that fits the Abandoned category. She is the single head of a household with three children ages ten, six and three. While she was in the process of getting a divorce from her husband, she went with her children to live with her sister. Mrs. Jones subsequently got a job as a store clerk and her AFDC check and childcare provision were discontinued. About the same time her ten year old daughter got chicken pox and was experiencing problems with asthma. The school would call Mrs. Jones about her daughter's asthma but the employer did not allow time off. This new job consequently lasted only one month.

Two months after moving in with her sister, the sister moved out. Mrs. Jones had no job, no child support and no money and had to tell her children they would all have to go to an emergency shelter. The children were "shocked" and still ask when they are going to move out of the shelter. Mrs. Jones has headaches that she says are related to the divorce. She says that it is harder to get a job when homeless but is planning to start a six-month class at a vocational institute because she wants to get a well paying job.

She said what would help her family the most is
getting into low-income housing.

For the Maintainers, the problems encountered were
ultimately found to be so overwhelming and unyielding that,
whether they accepted or resisted the loss of housing, all of these
families ended up homeless. All but one Abandoned family had
moved out, apparently without means to prevent it. The one
divorced and Abandoned family fought to keep their family home
but found that no matter how they tried, the single mother's
income could not pay for childcare and make mortgage payments.

Chapter IX:

Summary and Recommendations

SUMMARY

This study has taken a family focus on homelessness because the family is the foundation of society and is particularly vulnerable to the ravages of homelessness. The future of humanity depends on the wellbeing of families and their children, their values, skills, and abilities, and how well they are prepared to participate in family and community life and society.

This study suggests the condition of homeless families is, in general, much more difficult and complicated than that of homeless single adults. Families with children are composed of multiple individuals in reciprocal relationships involving trust, complete dependency, and responsibility. The very material needs of families are more extensive than that of individuals. They require more food, more clothes, more supplies, more housing, and more transportation. Young family members are found to have emotional, psychological, educational and caregiving requirements that are much more comprehensive and long lasting than those of adults. Because the basic needs of a family are more demanding and costly than of individuals, the family is at special risk and vulnerable to loss of income and homelessness. By its very nature the family has a vital role in nurturing children; it is consequently most important for society that families avoid the trauma of homelessness or recover quickly from its devastating effects.

The financial requirements of a family to attain self sufficiency are more profound than that of a single adult, yet the obstacles to achieving it are greater. Children require twenty-four hour care and most single parents have difficulty finding employment that will afford them daycare for the children in addition to rent and other expenses. Once homeless, it becomes even more difficult, yet more important, for the family to accumulate enough resources to re-establish housing, to provide for other essential needs and allow time and energy for caregiving responsibilities.

According to the data, the obvious and most basic and underlying cause of homelessness for all the families in the study was a lack of resources to either obtain or sustain adequate housing. How they arrived at that perilous condition varied. Before becoming homeless, the majority of the families were living below poverty level with a mean income of little more than $1000. But, they were "making it". Whether fitting the category of Improvers or Maintainers, all the families interviewed eventually ended up homeless because of being "vulnerable and having things happen". Events such as the loss of employment, medical problems, getting behind in bills or rent payments, not being able to obtain a job that would support a family were disastrous. Major life changes like birth, death or divorce, and not being able to find affordable housing, were all factors the families say contributed to their loss of housing. The majority of single parent Improver families became homeless trying to escape domestic violence or a drug abusing environment. Then, after getting away they found they could not obtain a job or housing.

After an exhaustive local job search, some families from out of state became homeless trying to better their lives by moving to a place where they could find a job and start over. This is the same motivation that caused migration during the great 1930s depression and one that is currently causing a healthy influx of new residents to the Pacific Northwest. For families in the study, this move proved to be the final stressor to their limited financial, emotional, and energy resources and they ended up in an emergency shelter.

Other families were found to have left their housing only when their situation deteriorated such that they were asked to leave. Some of these families resisted and fought to maintain their housing by a variety of means. When their efforts ultimately failed they also ended up on the street or in an emergency shelter.

Mental illness or emotional problems were not found to be a cause of homelessness for the families, but becoming homeless affected their mental health with an increase of stress and depression. Changes in mood and behavior were observed in the children, from infants to teenagers. Since becoming homeless, existing physical problems worsened for the families and new health problems developed.

As the study suggests, children did not and are not faring well through the experience of homelessness. Their lives and security have been disrupted and their reaction is anger, depression, resentment, and fear. Over one-fourth of the families did not have their school age children attending school. Of those families whose children did attend school, two-thirds went to the same schools as they did prior to becoming homeless. This is a finding not seen or discussed in reports on homeless children in other parts of the country. Behavior in school and out was negatively affected as was the behavior of younger children, with a marked regression to an earlier stage of development common.

Discharging the family care giving responsibilities was rendered more difficult for the majority of families. This finding is consistent with reports concerning the welfare hotel populations in New York (Kozel, 1987). Daily tasks such as washing clothes, acquiring food and fixing meals became much more complicated and onerous after becoming homeless. For a few families, who had been living in their cars or in extremely disruptive situations, caregiving was experienced as easier.

Although living in an emergency shelter proved to be very hard on the physical and emotional health of family members, the parents did appreciate having a place to be with their children. But, for the majority of families, one month in a shelter was not enough time to acquire sufficient resources to obtain new housing.

As some families reported, they were in shock. They tried to improve their situation and had failed; others did not even know where to start. The families knew their loss was more than just housing. It included parents' health, both physical and mental and that of their children. It involved lost self-esteem, self-respect, dignity and confidence. What ever the events that brought them to homelessness, rising above it seemed nearly impossible.

RECOMMENDATIONS

A vigorous program to prevent family homelessness and to help families that are already homeless would make the welfare of the American people a priority. A program to prevent homelessness would inform the public of the supports already available. When needed, it would provide the basic necessities of food, shelter, medical aid. When needed the government would assist the families to obtain jobs and with funding to get into housing. The condition, of not having adequate income to obtain or support family housing needs, brings sharply into focus the lack of suitable jobs and the paucity of affordable or low-income housing available.

The recommendations given by the families to prevent others from becoming homeless *first* and primarily concerns housing issues, specifically, increasing the supply of low-income housing. The *second* measure is to increase the number of jobs and job training so families will be better able to afford housing. The fact that families were asking for an increase in minimum wage indicates that some were trying to survive at this minimal wage. The *third* recommendation concerns making the welfare system more effective and functional for those who need it.

Families suggest that information be disseminated on how to avoid homelessness, on how to better manage money and to make people aware of the programs already available. The families advise that more legal aid be provided at low or no cost for low-income people and stiffer penalties be imposed for violence and abuse. To prevent homelessness, counseling should be available for whatever problems the families have, including substance abuse.

To assist families that are already homeless the list is similar but more extensive. The families recommend the provision of more emergency shelters and more funding for food and clothing. They suggest allowing longer stays in shelters or an increase in interim housing programs to provide transition between emergency shelter and regular housing. This would permit the homeless family time to save up money and get on their feet. The families saw counseling was as essential for both children and adults, from individual therapy to financial counseling.

To return families to a more stable life, they recommend that the government increase the amount of housing, especially low cost housing. Families suggest providing low-income housing with set-asides for homeless families and giving more information to apartment owners on the Section Eight program. The families think it is necessary to give assistance to families to get into housing. To assist the homeless, they think government needs to provide more jobs and job training to enable homeless families to become self sufficient. The families say it is important to raise the minimum wage and provide affordable childcare programs with childcare available during the job search and after. The families also recommended increasing the welfare benefits for those who need it.

UNEXPECTED FINDINGS

The most unanticipated and surprising finding was the number of families who left their housing voluntarily in a bold attempt to improve their situation before it worsened. The fact that over half of the families in this sample fit that condition, made it seem obvious that this was a factor that should not be ignored. Based on this sample population, a typology was developed that looked cursorily at the initiating behavior and coping styles of families facing adversity and under threat of losing their housing.

The significance of this finding and the proposed typology may be in the clues it provides for designing programs that would target specific populations, at risk of becoming homeless in predictable ways. Although becoming homeless may be a leveler of aspiration, confidence, and energy; finding differences in coping styles and initiating behaviors before becoming homeless may help in identifying how best to assist those families already homeless.

LIMITATIONS OF THE RESEARCH

The focus of this study was limited to interviews of homeless families about their situation prior to and after becoming homeless as well as their recommendations for services and policy changes.

1. This research did not look into the issues of the housing market, neither the numbers of low-income housing units lost over the last ten years nor the market rates that make housing difficult or impossible for low-income families, although these subjects do have a direct bearing on family homelessness.
2. This study did not focus on employment issues neither the number of jobs available that could be obtained without specialized training nor whether such jobs could support a family, although this turned out to be a major concern for the families.
3. This study did not address the availability of low cost daycare for children although the lack of it was regarded by the families as a barrier to employment.

The generalizability of the findings of this study to other homeless families is restricted by the fact that:

1. The families were surveyed at one time during the year. They and their experiences may not be representative of homeless families found at other times and places.
2. The families interviewed may be different from other homeless families that did not survive the shelter- screening process. Information on how many families were screened out and for what reasons was not available.
3. No non-English speaking family was interviewed.
4. Not all guests of the shelters present during the time period of the survey were available to be interviewed. The families not interviewed were reportedly those whose stays were too

short or who were too busy "taking care of business". These families may differ from those interviewed in that they were less immobilized by their situation and were therefore more aggressive or capable of handling or getting out of their situation.

5. Only two shelters out of an estimated fourteen in the area were surveyed. The largest family shelter, a mission, as well as some of the smaller ones may have housed a slightly different population, with motivations, character traits, and experiences different than the one interviewed.

6. Researchers have found that offering money to those in great need may subtly influence them to participate This may in turn may have biased their responses. All answers to very personal problems were taken at face value.

7. As a self protection mechanism Families may not have been completely honest in their response to questions about conditions or behaviors they thought would be disapproved of or censored, such as, mental illness or drug use.

8. The study was conducted at one point in time. Due to the nature of homelessness, there was no opportunity do to a longitudinal study of these families.

STATEWIDE STUDY COMPARISON

A survey regarding homelessness across Washington State was undertaken eleven months later in November 1988 by the Washington State Department of Community Development in conjunction with the Washington Coalition for the Homeless. The survey questionnaire was sent to and filled out by providers and guests of all state recognized and state supported emergency shelters. The instrument for shelter guests *duplicates* parts of the questionnaire used in this earlier family survey. The preliminary findings of the statewide survey substantiates some general findings of the family study under discussion indicating that this was not just a shot in time; the problem persists.

The ages of the adults in the families are in the same range; the education level of the adults also fits the same profile. The ethnic composition of the statewide study shows more Whites and less Blacks than the family study. This may be explained in part by the fact that according to the state study most racial minorities are found in the larger metropolitan areas, such as where the family study was done.

The reasons for homelessness were the same as those cited in the family study with new to the area cited first for two-parent families followed by lost job and no money for rent. For single parent families the first reason was leaving violence, followed by unsuccessful doubling up with others and new to the area, divorce, no rent money and eviction. The state study provided a check list with no prioritization of responses asked for.

The state study indicates five percent of the two-parent families and thirteen percent of the single-parent families report hospitalization for mental illness. This was not reported in the family study. An indication of drug and alcohol problems and involvement in treatment was also seen in the state study as it was in the family study.

In the statewide study, approximately forty percent of the families gave a street address as the last place they lived before becoming homeless. In the family study, a corresponding percentage of families reported the shelter where they were interviewed was the first one they had stayed in. Sixty percent of families in the state study gave the same variety of temporary accommodations for their previous living situation. They listed friends/family, other shelter, car, streets, and camping. The number of shelters stayed in the previous two years is very similar to that found in the family study. The barriers to finding housing are reportedly the same with no rent money listed first followed closely by no job. A lack of daycare for children was considered to be the most overwhelming barrier to finding and keeping jobs for families in the statewide study. This was especially so for single-parent families.

NEW AREAS OF RESEARCH

In general, more research is needed on programs to prevent homelessness, including more detailed research about the motivations and coping behaviors of families that may influence their becoming homeless and may influence their coping behaviors. Follow-up studies are needed on the effects of homelessness on children and families and how to best meet the needs of families to ameliorate the devastating effects of homelessness.

It is hypothesized that being aware of differences in the causes of families becoming homeless and in their coping behaviors may ultimately help in planning programs to prevent families from becoming homeless. In addition to understanding the commonality of causes, addressing their diverse needs and situations may prevent families from ending up in that condition. As a key to assisting the families to survive the experience of being homeless, it may also be important or relevant to determine family characteristics and their usual mode of operating and coping style. In order to do this, in depth studies exploring the various categories of the typology, discussed in Chapter VII, are recommended.

A longitudinal study could be undertaken that would first assess or determine the family behavioral or coping styles at initial contact for services. This would take place ideally when the family was first undergoing serious financial problems, such as a loss of job and before loss of housing. The families would then be followed over time including through homelessness if it came to that. The goal would be to see if different coping styles help them through their crisis in any significant way. Indicators might be a shorter length of time of time in crisis or less trauma or damage to the well being of adults or children.

A separate or companion study could be undertaken to see if different kinds of financial help, supportive counseling, or classes would be of more assistance to shorten the time of need or dependency. It is hypothesized that for some families a lump sum of money would allow them to "get on their feet" and become self supporting much more quickly than minimal support over a longer period of time. For other families a lesser amount of money over time, to assist them while they acquired some personal or living skills or job related competence, may be preferable. These latter research projects regarding assistance to homeless families could also be used to test the typology to see if families with different behavioral or coping styles are more successful with one type of assistance than another.

This study leaves these families in the shelter, some just arriving, some with their allotted time nearing completion, being told to move on to make room for others who also need a chance. Although this was reported to be the first shelter stay for forty percent of the families, the other sixty percent had not been able to make it out of homelessness in the past with just one shelter stay. No one knows how long it will take the families to become self sufficient or even if they will. A program of services is needed to follow these families to ensure their children's wellbeing and help them develop and escape from poverty. A model for this type of program would involve permanent-type low cost housing and case management services as requested or needed.

Several demonstration programs to house homeless families have been funded in the past with the goal of assisting families to become stable and self reliant. This willingness to address the problems of the homeless are to be acknowledged and encouraged. Recently elected President Bush spoke to a home builders convention in Texas and encouraged them to address the need for more low-income housing. There is a plan to increase the minimum wage over the next three years. The amount of the increase recommended is not adequate to support a family but this action shows movement in a positive direction.

Questionnaire

Date_____   Site _____

1.   How long have you been at this shelter? _____
_____

2.   Is this the first shelter that your family has stayed in? _____
_____
_____

3.   How long ago were you in your own apartment or house? _
_____

4.   Where were you living at that time?
City _____   State_____

5.   How much time passed from when you lost your apartment
or house until you stayed in an emergency shelter? _____
_____

6.   List the shelters you have stayed in during the last three
years?

Name	Location	Date

7.   How long do you think you need to stay in a shelter? _____

_____

_____

8.   Did you live in any other state or area of this state since becoming homeless? _____

_____

_____

9.   If yes, for what reasons did you move to Seattle? _____

_____

_____

10.   Please list the three most important reasons/problems that contributed to your becoming homeless. _____

_____

_____

_____

11.   What did you do to keep from losing your housing? _____

_____

_____

_____

12.   Were your children aware of what was happening? _____

_____

13.   If yes, what was their reaction? _____

_____

_____

_____

14.   How did you respond to their questions? _____

_____

_____

_____

15.   What else was going on in your life at this time? _____

_____

_____

_____

_____

_____

16.   Did you have to give up or sell any of your belongings such as your car, furniture, or clothes to keep your housing for a while longer? _____

_____

17.   Did you tell relatives or friends about losing your housing?

_____

_____

18.   Were they able to help? _____

_____

_____

_____

19.   What was the final problem or "last straw" that caused you to become homeless? _____

_____

_____

_____

_____

20.   What do you think would have been most helpful to prevent you and your family from becoming homeless? _____

_____

_____

_____

_____

21. *In general*, if the government was able to design a program to prevent families from becoming homeless what should it include? _____

_____

_____

_____

_____

22. *In general*, if help was available for only one problem, for what one problem do you think is the most important to get help?

_____

_____

_____

23. Do you have school-age children? _____

_____

_____

24. Are they presently enrolled in school? _____

_____

_____

25. Are they attending school on a regular basis? _____

_____

_____

26. Were they able to continue in the same school? _____

_____

_____

27. Have their grades or behavior at school changed since becoming homeless? _____

_____

_____

_____

28.   Have any of your children repeated a grade since becoming homeless? _____

29.   Have their behaviors or activities outside of school changed? _____

_____

_____

30.   Do you have preschool children? _____

_____

31.   Have their behaviors or activities changed since becoming homeless? _____

_____

_____

32.   What has been the major effect on your family, including your children, of becoming homeless? _____

_____

_____

_____

_____

33.   Are you the primary care giver for your children, (e.g. fix meals, wash clothes, take care of them when sick, etc.)? _____

_____

_____

_____

34.   Are you the care giver for any other members of your family (e.g. parents, etc.)? _____

_____

_____

35.   Have the difficulties in taking care of your family changed since becoming homeless? _____

If yes, please explain.

_____

_____

_____

_____

36.   Did you or anyone in your immediate family have health problems that affected your ability to solve your housing? _____

_____

37.   If yes, which person(s) in your family had the problem? ___

_____

_____

_____

38.   How did this illness affect your time? _____

_____

_____

      money? _____

_____

      energy? _____

_____

39.   Has becoming homeless affected your family's physical health, i.e. has your family experienced more illness or injuries?

_____

_____

_____

_____

40.   Was mental illness or the emotional problems of a family member something that affected your family's ability to cope with housing problems or keep housing? _____

_____

_____

_____

_____

41. Has becoming homeless affected your family's mental health? _____

_____

_____

_____

42. Has becoming homeless affected your employment or your job opportunities? _____

_____

_____

_____

43. What is your (and/or your partner's) regular kind of work?
(self)_____ (partner) _____

44. Are you (or your partner) unemployed at this time?
(self)_____ (partner) _____

45. How long has it been since you have had steady stable employment?
(self)_____ (partner) _____

46. If a job became available would you work? _____

_____

47. For what reasons would you not work? _____

_____

_____

_____

48. Did you use daycare for your children before you became homeless? _____

_____

_____

_____

49. Before becoming homeless what was your income?
$_____/mo.

50. From what source(s)? (e.g. employment, AFDC, etc.) ____

_____

_____

_____

_____

51. Were you able to keep up with paying your bills on a regular basis?_____If no, please explain. _____

_____

_____

_____

52. Were government or private assistance programs used by your family before becoming homeless? (e.g. AFDC, SSI, Medicare, Medicaid, VA benefits, Food Stamps, food banks, low-income utility assistance, etc.) _____

_____

_____

_____

_____

53. What is your present income? $_____/mo

54. From what source(s)? (e.g. employment, AFDC, etc.) ____

_____

_____

_____

_____

55. Was divorce a problem that contributed to you and your children becoming homeless? _____ If yes, please explain ___

_____

_____

_____

56. Is domestic violence or abuse a problem for your family? __

_____

_____

57. If yes, how long had this abuse or violence been going on?

_____

_____

58. Did becoming homeless result in an increase or decrease of child or spousal abuse in your family? _____

_____

_____

59. Have problems of family violence caused you to seek emergency shelter? _____

_____

_____

60. What factors, if any, do you consider as elements that contributed to the increase of violence by the abuser? _____

_____

_____

_____

_____

61. Did alcohol or drug use contribute to your becoming homeless? _____

_____

_____

62. Has alcohol or drug use in your family changed (increased or decreased) since you became homeless? _____

_____

If yes, please explain _____

_____

_____

_____

63. Do you think that you or your children need or would benefit by receiving counseling to help overcome some of the problems related to being homeless?_____

_____

64. If yes, please describe what kind of counseling you think would be helpful. (e.g. emotional or, school, marital, drug, alcohol, employment, financial, housing, etc.)_____

_____

_____

_____

_____

65. What would help your family the most to get back into secure, stable housing?_____

_____

_____

_____

_____

66. *In general*, if you were asked to give government officials or program managers your ideas on how to design a program to help families that are already homeless, what suggestions would you have?_____

_____

_____

_____

_____

FAMILY DEMOGRAPHICS

Number of adults_____   Number of children _____
Marital status _____

	ID Number	Age	Sex	Race	Education
Adult	_____	__	_	_____	_____
Adult	_____	__	_	_____	_____
Child	_____	__	_	_____	_____
Child	_____	__	_	_____	_____
Child	_____	__	_	_____	_____
Child	_____	__	_	_____	_____
Child	_____	__	_	_____	_____
Child	_____	__	_	_____	_____

ID Number = first 2 letters of last name, first two letters of first name, day of birth (e.g. 01, 24 etc.) and month of birth (01–12).

Interview Consent Form

for Interviews of Homeless Families
with Young Children,
University of Washington

Investigator: Angie van Ry, Doctoral Candidate
School of Social Work, 543-5640

PURPOSES AND BENEFITS

This is a study about homeless families with children. We do not yet know very much about why families become homeless or what effect being homeless has on families and children. Learning how families are affected by not having a home will enable us to better help those families that are already homeless to overcome their problems and get "back on their feet" into regular or stable housing. Information about the many ways families end up losing their home will help us to design services to prevent families from becoming homeless.

To get the kind of information about homeless families that will be helpful we will be asking you, as the head of household or adult female in the family, some questions. Your answers may enable us to provide your family with additional services now while you are in this shelter or later by connecting you to other services available in the community. The interview will take a little more than an hour. For your help we will pay you ten dollars.

This study is being conducted in partial fulfillment of the requirements for a graduate degree in the School of Social Work.

RISKS, STRESS, DISCOMFORT

Because being homeless affects a family's personal or private life, there will be some questions about sensitive issues such as alcohol or drug use or family conflict or violence. If these questions cause you discomfort and you feel that you would like counseling, we will make certain it is available to you at no cost. Participation in this study is entirely voluntary and you are free to skip any question or to quit at any time. Your participation in the study will not affect the services you are presently getting at this shelter.

Information from these interviews will be put together in a report which will be given to government and agency officials who are trying to find ways to prevent families from becoming homeless and ways to help families that are already homeless. The results of the research will also be placed in the thesis section of the University of Washington Library.

Your answers will be kept confidential. Only the researcher will have access to the interview information. The one exception to the confidentiality of the research data is that the law requires that suspected cases of child abuse be reported to Children's Protective Services. Your name will not appear on the questionnaire. These forms will be destroyed in three years.

PARTICIPANT'S STATEMENT

I have read this consent form and have had the opportunity to ask questions and have them answered. I voluntarily consent to participate. I understand that future questions I may have about the research or about subjects' rights will be answered by the investigator listed above. I understand that I can withdraw from participating at any time and may skip answering any questions that I choose.

_____

Signature of Participant   Date

_____

Signature of Interviewer   Date

Shelter _____

Copies to: Subject
                 Investigator's file

Bibliography

Ackley, Sheldon. 1978. "A Right to Subsistence." *Social Policy* 28 No. 2: 3–11.

Anderson, S.C., Boe, T., and Smith, S. 1988. "Homeless Women." *Affilia* 3 No. 2: 62–70.

Bachrach, L.L. 1984. "Interpreting Research on the Homeless Mentally Ill: Some Caveats." *Hospital and Community Psychiatry* 35: 914–917.

Bahr, H.M. 1967. "The Gradual Disappearance of Skid Row." *Social Policy* 15, No. 1: 41–45

Bahr, H.M. 1973. *Skid row: An Introduction to Disaffiliation.* New York: Oxford University Press.

Bahr, H.M. and Garrett, Gerald R. 1976. *Women Alone: The Disaffiliation of Urban Women.* Lexington, MA: Lexington Books.

Bassuk, E.L. 1985. "The Feminization of Homelessness: Homeless Families in Boston Shelters." Keynote address given at Shelter, Inc.'s yearly benefit, July 1, Harvard Science Center, Cambridge, MA.

Bassuk. E.L. 1986. "Homeless." *People Magazine*, March: 86–88.

Bassuk, E.L. 1986. "Homeless Families: Single Mothers and Their Children in Boston Shelters." In *The Mental Health Needs of Homeless Persons,* ed. E.L. Bassuk, pp. 45–54. New Directions for Mental Health Services 30. San Francisco: Jossey-Bass, Inc.

Bassuk, E.L., Rubin, L., and Lauriat, A. 1986. "Characteristics of Sheltered Homeless Families." *American Journal of Public Health* 76, No. 9: 1097–1101.

Bassuk, E.L. 1988. "Why Does Family Homelessness Occur? A Case-Control Study." *American Journal of Public Health* 78, No. 7: 783–788.

Baxter, E. and Hopper, K. 1981. *Private Lives/Public Spaces: Homeless Adults on the Streets of New York City.* New York: Community Service Society.

Bingham, R.D., Green, R.E. and White, A.B. eds. 1987. *The Homeless in Contemporary Society.* Newbury Park, CA: Sage.

Borgos, S. 1984. "The Acorn Squatters' Campaign." *Social Policy,* Summer: 17–26.

Breakey, W.R. and Fisher, P.J. 1975. "Down and Out in the Land of Plenty." *Johns Hopkins Magazine,* June: 16–24.

Brickner, P.W. 1985. *Health Care of Homeless People.* New York: Springer Publishing Co.

Brown, J. 1940. *Public Relief.* Washington, DC: U.S. Government Printing Office.

Carliner, M.S. 1987. "Homelessness: A Housing Problem?" In *The Homeless in Contemporary Society,* ed. R.D. Bingham, R.E. Green, and S.B. White, pp. 119–128. Newbury Park, CA: Sage.

Caton, C.L.M. 1986. "The Homeless Experience in Adolescent Years." In *The Mental Health Needs of Homeless Persons,* ed. E.L. Bassuk, pp. 63–70. New Directions for Mental Health Services 30. San Francisco: Jossey-Bass Inc.

Church Council of Greater Seattle. 1987. *Homelessness: The Growing Crisis.* Seattle: Author.

Coalition for the Homeless. 1984. *Perchance to Sleep: Homeless Children Without Shelter in New York City.* New York: Author.

Corrigan, E. 1984. "Homeless Alcoholic Women on Skid Row." *American Journal of Drug and Alcohol Abuse* 10: 535–549.

Crystal, S. 1984. "Homeless Men and Homeless Women: The Gender Gap." *Urban and Social Change Review* 17, No. 2.

Davis, M. 1984. "Forced to Tramp: The Perspective of the Labor Press." In *Walking to Work,* ed. E.H. Monkkonen. Lincoln: University of Nebraska Press.

Erickson, J. and Wilhelm, C. eds. 1986. *Housing the Homeless.* New Jersey: Center for Urban Policy Research.

First, R.J., Roth, D., and Arewa, B.D. 1988. "Homelessness: Understanding the Dimensions of the Problem for Minorities." *Social Work* 33: 120–124.

Frazier, S.H. 1985. "Responding to the Needs of the Homeless Mentally Ill." *Public Health Reports* 100, No. 5: 462-469.

Gewirtzman, R. and Fodor, I. 1987. "The Homeless Child at School: From Welfare Hotel to Classroom." *Child Welfare* 66: 237–245.

Goldman, H.H. and Morrissey, J.P. 1985. "The Alchemy of Mental Health Policy: Homelessness and the Fourth Cycle of Reform." *American Journal of Public Health* 75, No. 7: 727–731.

Goode, S. 1987. "Homeless Find Shelter in the Courts." *Insight* 3, No. 7: 56–57.

Governor's Advisory Board on the Shelter, Nutrition and Service Program for Homeless Persons. 1986. *Homelessness: Recommendations for State Action.* Maryland: Author.

Hagen, J.L. 1987. "The Heterogeneity of Homelessness". *Social Casework* 68: 451–457.

Hagen, J.L. and Ivanoff, A.M. 1988. "Homeless Women: A High-risk Population." *Affilia* 3, No. 1: 19–33.

Hartman, C. 1986. "The Housing Part of the Homelessness Problem." In *The Mental Health Needs of Homeless Persons,* ed. E.L. Bassuk, pp. 71–86. New Directions for Mental Health Services 30. San Francisco: Jossey-Bass Inc.

Hayes, R.M. 1984. Testimony before the House Intergovernmental Relations and Human Resources Subcommittee of the Committee on Government Operations from *Perchance to Sleep: Homeless Children Without Shelter in New York City.* New York: Coalition for the Homeless.

Hechinger, F.M. 1987. "Plight of the Homeless." *The New York Times,* May 5, p. 27.

Hoch, C. 1987. "A Brief History of the Homeless Problem in the United States." In *The Homeless in Contemporary Society,* ed. R.D. Bingham, R.E. Green, and S.B. White, pp. 16–33. Newbury Park, CA: Sage.

Hoch, C. and Slayton, R. 1989. *New Homeless and Old: Community and the Skid Row Hotel*. PA: Temple University Press

Hombs, M.E. and Snyder, M. 1983. *Homelessness in America: A Forced March to Nowhere.*. 2nd ed. Washington, D.C.: Community for Creative Non-violence.

"Homeless kids: 'Forgotten Faces'." 1986. *Newsweek* January 6.

Homelessness Information Exchange. 1988. *Family and Child Homelessness,* April. Washington, D.C.: Homelessness Information Exchange Service.

"Homeless Population Increasing Dramatically Nationwide." 1989. *Safety Network,* October.

Hope, M. and Young, J. 1986. *The Faces of Homelessness*. Massachusetts: Lexington Books.

Hopper, K. 1983. "Homelessness: Reducing the Distance." *New England Journal of Human Services,* Fall: 30-47.

Hopper, K. and Hamberg, J. 1984. *The Making of America's Homeless: From Skid Row to New Poor 1945-1984*. New York: Community Service Society of New York.

Human Resources Coalition. 1984. *Emergency Shelter Study in Seattle/King County.* King County, WA: Dept. Housing and Community Development.

Hutchison, W.J., Searight, P., and Stretch, J.J. 1986. "Multidimensional Networking: A Response to the Needs of Homeless Families." *Social Work* 31: 427–430.

Institute of Medicine. 1988. *Homelessness, Health, and Human Needs.* Washington DC: Institute of Medicine.

Jahiel, R.I. 1987. "The Situation of the Homeless." In *The Homeless in Contemporary Society,* ed. R.D. Bingham, R.E. Green, and S.B. White, pp.99–118. Newbury Park, CA: Sage.

Jirovec, R. 1984. "Documenting the Impact of Reaganomics on Social Welfare Recipients." *Arete* 9, No. 1: 36–47.

Johnson, A.K. 1988. *A Survey of the St. Louis Area Emergency Shelters for the Homeless.* August. Homeless Services Network Board.

Johnson, A.K. 1989. *Community Planning for the Homeless: Has Anything Changed in Sixty Years?* Paper presented at the annual program meeting of the Council on Social Work Education, March, Chicago, IL.

Johnson, A.K. 1989. "Female-headed Homeless Families: A Comparative Profile." *Affilia* 4, No. 4: 23–39.

Kaufman, N. 1984. "Homelessness: A Comprehensive Policy Approach." *Urban and Social Change Review* 17, No. 1: 21–26.

Kearney, S. 1985. "A Hot Meal, Warm Clothes and a Place to Sleep: America's Homeless." *CSG Backgrounder.* No. 038502, pp.1–7. Lexington: The Council of State Governments.

King County Housing and Community Development. 1986. *Homelessness Revisited: 1986 Seattle-King County Emergency Shelter Study Update.* King County, WA: Author.

Kondratus, S.A. 1986. "A Strategy for Helping America's Homeless." In *Housing the Homeless,* ed. J. Erickson and C. Wilhelm, pp. 144–149. New Jersey: Center for Urban Policy Research.

Kozol, J. 1988a. "The Homeless and Their Children—I." *The New Yorker,* January 25: 65+.

Kozol, J. 1988b. "The Homeless and Their Children—II." *The New Yorker,* February 1: 36+.

Kozol, J. 1988c. *Rachel and Her Children: Homeless Families in America.* New York: Crown.

Langdon, J.K. and Kass, M. 1985. "Homelessness in America: Looking for the Right to Shelter." *Columbia Journal of Law and Social Problems* 19: 305–392.

Lamb H.R., ed. 1984. *The Homeless Mentally Ill: a Task Force Report of the American Psychiatric Association.* Washington D.C.: Am. Psych. Assoc.

Lauriat, A.S. 1986. "Sheltering Homeless Families: Beyond an Emergency Response." In *The Mental Health Needs of Homeless Persons,* ed. E.L. Bassuk, pp. 87–94. New Directions for Mental Health Services 30. San Francisco: Jossey-Bass Inc.

League of Women Voters of Seattle. 1985. *Children in Our City: Children at Risk: Street Youth*. Seattle: League of Women Voters of Seattle.

Leavitt, J. and Saegert, S. 1984. "Women and Abandoned Buildings: A Feminist Approach to Housing." *Social Policy*, Summer: 32–39.

Leepson, M. 1982. "The Homeless: Growing National Problem." *Editorial Research Reports* 2: 793–812.

Lochhead, C. 1988. "All Alone, With No Home." *Insight* 4, No. 20: 12–15.

Lochhead, C. 1988. "Door Opening To Dignity." *Insight* 4, No. 20: 16–18.

Lochhead, C. 1988. "Nowhere To Go, Always In Sight." *Insight* 4, No. 20: 8–11.

Malcom, A.H. 1986). "Record Numbers of the Homeless Seeking Aid in the Nation's Cities." *The New York Times*, October 30, pp. 1+.

Marin, P. 1987. "Helping and Hating the Homeless." *Harpers Magazine*, January: 39–49.

Massinga, R. 1986. *Where Do You Go From Nowhere: Homelessness In Maryland*. Maryland: Department of Human Resources, Public Information Office.

Mathews, J. 1985. "The Homeless." *The Washington Post* 2, No. 45: 6–8.

Maza, P.L. and Hall, J.A. 1988. *Homeless Children and Their Families: A Preliminary Study*. Washington, DC: Child Welfare League of America.

McGerigle, P. and Louriat, A. 1983. *More Than a Shelter: A Community Response to Homelessness, (Report and Recommendations)*. Massachusetts Association for Mental Health.

McSheey, W. 1979. *Skid Row*. Cambridge, MA: Schenkman.

Miller, D.S. 1985. (definitions of homelessness) prepared for the Homeless Families Project. University of Washington.

Miller, D.S. and Lin, E.H. 1988. "Children in Sheltered Homeless Families: Reported Health Status and Use of Health Services." *Pediatrics* 81: 668–673.

Monkkonen, E.H., ed. 1984. *Walking to Work.* Lincoln: University of Nebraska Press.

National Coalition for the Homeless. 1988. "Oklahoma's Homeless Face Crisis: Advocates Battle Current Myths." *Safety Network* 6, No. 4: 4.

Orenstein, A. and Phillips, W. 1978. *Understanding Social Research: An Introduction.* Boston: Allyn and Bacon Inc.

Pear, R. 1986. "The Need of the Nation's Homeless is Becoming Their Right. *The New York Times,* July 20, p. E 5.

Phillips, M.H., DeChillo, N., Kronenfeld, D., and Middleton-Jeter, V. 1988. "Homeless Families: Services Make a Difference. *Social Casework.* January: 48–53.

Phillips, M.H., Kronenfeld, D., and Jeter, V. 1986. "A Model of Services to Homeless Families in Shelters." In *Housing the Homeless,* ed. J. Erickson and C. Wilhelm. New Jersey: Center for Urban Policy Research.

Redburn, F.S., and Buss. T.F. 1986. *Responding to America's Homeless: Public Policy Alternatives.* New York: Praeger.

Riis, J.A. 1971. *How the Other Half Lives.* New York: Dover.

Rivlin, L.G. 1986. "A New Look at the Homeless." *Social Policy.* 3–10.

Rhoden, N.K. 1982. "The Limits of Liberty: Deinstitutionalization, Homelessness and Libertarian Theory." *Emory Law Journal* 31, No. 2: 375–440.

Robertson, M.J. 1986. "Mental Disorder Among Homeless Persons in the United States: An Overview of Recent Empirical Literature." *Administration in Mental Health* 14, No. 1: 14–27.

Ropers, R.H. 1988. *The Invisible Homeless: A New Urban Ecology.* New York: Human Sciences Press.

Rossi, P.H., Fisher, G.A., and Willis, G. 1986. *The Condition of the Homeless of Chicago.* Amherst: University of Massachusetts, Social and Demographic Research Institute.

Roth, D. and Bean, J. 1985. *Homelessness in Ohio: A Study of People in Need.* Ohio Department of Mental Health, Office of Program Evaluation and Research.

Ryback, R.F., and Bassuk, E.L. 1986. "Homeless Battered Women and Their Shelter Network. In *The Mental Health*

Needs of Homeless Persons, ed. E. L. Bassuk, pp. 55–62. New Directions for Mental Health Services 30. San Francisco: Jossey-Bass Inc.

Salerno, D., Hopper, K., Baxter, E. 1984. *Hardship in the Heartland: Homelessness in Eight Cities.* New York: Community Service Society of New York.

Schneider, J. 1984. "Tramping Workers, 1890-1920: A Subcultural View." In *Walking to Work,* ed. E.H. Monkkonen. Lincoln: University of Nebraska Press.

Simpson, J.H., Kilduff, M., and Blewett, C.D. 1984. *Struggling to Survive in a Welfare Hotel.* New York: Community Service Society.

Smith, N. 1985. "Homelessness: Not One Problem, But Many." *The Journal of the Institute for Socioeconomic Studies* 10, No. 3.

Snow, D.A., Baker, S.G., Anderson, L., and Martin, M. 1986. "The Myth of Mental Illness Among the Homeless. *Social Problems* 33: 407–423.

Sprague, J.F. Hayashi, R., Krapf, A., Wallen, S. and Stein, S. 1986. *A Manual On Transitional Housing.* Boston: Women's Institute for Housing and Economic Dev., Inc.

Stefl, M.E. 1987. "The New Homeless: A National Perspective." In *The Homeless in Contemporary Society,* ed. R.D. Bingham, R.E. Green, and White, S.B., pp. 46–63. Newbury Park, CA: Sage.

Stern, M.J. 1984. "The Emergence of the Homeless As A Public Problem." *Social Service Review* 58: 291–301.

Steiner, G.Y. 1966. *Social Insecurity: The Politics of Welfare.* Chicago: Rand McNally.

Stoddard, P.H. 1985. "Changes in Presidential Perceptions of the Problem of Unemployment." *Journal of Applied Social Sciences* 9, No. 1: 1–25.

Stoner, M.R. 1983. "An Analysis of Public and Private Sector Provisions for the Homeless." *Urban and Social Change Review* 17, No. 1: 3–8.

Stoner, M.R. 1983. "The Plight of Homeless Women." *Social Science Review* 57: 291–301.

Sub-committee on the Constitution. 1980. *Homeless Youth: The Saga of 'Pushouts' and 'Throwaways' in America.* Washington D.C.: US Gov. Printing Office.

Sullivan, P.A. and Damrosch, S.P. 1987. "Homeless Women and Children." In *The Homeless in Contemporary Society,* ed. R.D. Bingham, R.E. Green, and S.B. White, pp. 82–98. Newbury Park, CA: Sage.

Surber, R.W., Dwyer, E., Ryan. K.J., Goldfinger, S.M., and Kelly, J.T. 1988. "Medical and Psychiatric Needs of the Homeless—A Preliminary Response. *Social Work* 33: 116–119.

Tizon, A. 1989. The myths of poverty debunked. *The Seattle Times,* October 10, p A1+.

Tygiel, J. 1984. "Tramping Artisans: Carpenters in Industrial America." In *Walking to Work,* ed. E.H. Monkkonen Lincoln: University of Nebraska Press.

United States Conference of Mayors. 1984. *Status Report: Emergency Food, Shelter, and Energy Programs in 20 Cities.* Washington D.C.: Author.

United States Conference of Mayors. 1982. *Status Report: Homelessness.* Washington D.C.: Author.

United States Conference of Mayors. 1987. *The Continuing Growth of Hunger, Homelessness, and Poverty in America's Cities: 1987.* Washington D.C.: Author.

United States House of Representatives, Committee on Government Operations. 1986. *Homeless Families: A Neglected Crisis.* Washington D.C.: U.S. Printing Office.

United States House of Representatives, Select Committee on Children, Youth and Families. 1987. *The Crisis in Homelessness: Effects On Children and Families.* Washington D.C.: U.S. Printing Office.

United States Department of Housing and Urban Development, Office of Policy Development and Research. 1984. *A Report to the Secretary On Homelessness and Emergency Shelters.* Washington D.C.: US Printing Office.

United States General Accounting Office. 1985. *Homelessness: A Complex Problem and the Federal Response.* Washington D.C.: US Gov. Printing Office.

van Ry, A. 1988. "Meeting the Needs of Homeless Families in a Complex Society." Paper presented at the annual program meeting of the Council on Social Work Education, March, Chicago, IL.

Wackstein, N. 1983. *No One's In Charge: Homeless Families With Children in Temporary Shelter.* New York: Citizens Committee for Children of New York Inc.

Wackstein, N. 1984. *7000 Homeless Children: The Crisis Continues.* New York: Citizens Committee for Children of New York Inc.

Wallace, S.E. 1965. *Skid Row As A Way of Life.* Totowa, N.J.: Bedminister Press.

Webb J.N. 1935. *The Transient Unemployed.* Washington D.C.: Works Progress Administration.

Weigard, R.B. 1985. "Counting the Homeless." *American Demographics* 7: 34–37.

Whittemore, H. 1988. "We Can't Pay the Rent." *Parade Magazine*, January 10, pp. 4-6.

Wilson, R.S. 1935. "Problems in Coordinating Service for Transient and Resident Unattached From the Point of View of Individual Service." In *Report of the National Conference of Social Work, Montreal*, pp. 210–223.

Wolch, J.R. and Gabriel, S.A. 1985. "Dismantling the Community Based System." *Journal of the American Planning Association* 51, No. 2: 53–62.

Wright, J.D., Weber-Burden, E. Knight, J.W., and Lam, J.A. 1987. *The National Health Care for the Homeless Program: The First Year.* Amherst: University of Massachusetts, Social and Demographic Research Institute.